Shirley Temple Dolls and Fashions

A Collector's Guide To The World's Darling

by Edward R. Pardella

Schiffer Publishing Ltd

1469 Morstein Road, West Chester, Pennsylvania 19380

Dedication

For my Aunt Kitty, who taught me that "it's never too late to have a happy childhood." And for giving me a lifetime of love and understanding, I will always be grateful.

For Joseph, thanks for everything!

Printed in the United States of America.
ISBN: 0-88740-420-0

Published by Schiffer Publishing, Ltd.
1469 Morstein Road
West Chester, Pennsylvania 19380
Please write for a free catalog.
This book may be purchased from the publisher.
Please include $2.00 postage.
Try your bookstore first.

We are interested in hearing from authors with book ideas on related topics.

Contents

Acknowledgments

For supplying photographs and for their continued help and support, special thanks to:
Carole Barboza; G. Robert Brown, photography; Rosemary Dent; Muriel Dumais; Lorna
Erb; Helen Hesson; Marge Meisinger; Laura Terrace; and Glorya Woods.

Preface

An unexplained desire to mend or fulfill a lost childhood dream, or the rekindling of a treasured time long ago, are common themes which seem to surface time and again when you ask a collector why he or she collects. Add to that the enormous array of collectibles made in the image of, or bearing the name of, Shirley Temple, the most beloved child star of all time, and you will find a passion and commitment to collecting that is almost unequaled.

With the introduction of the Shirley Temple doll in 1934, the children of the 1930s suddenly found a way not only to emulate their childhood idol, but to actually have their very own Shirley Temple to love and care for. Like Shirley herself, the original Shirley Temple dolls were greatly treasured and admired. For the most part, they were always played with very carefully, and usually only on special occasions, not only because of whom they represented, but because of the high cost of purchasing the doll. Original prices ranged from $1.79 to $11.79, a hefty sum for the average family to pay for a toy in the early post depression era, especially if parents had many mouths to feed and many childhood dreams to try and satisfy.

One collector, who's parents were unable to afford their daughter a Shirley Temple doll, was Rosemary Dent, now a retired first grade teacher from West Virginia. Rosemary's enormous generosity in supplying photographs and information has helped make this book possible. During an early correspondence, she shared the following.

"Like so many Shirley Temple fans and doll collectors, I was a child of the depression who never had, but yearned for, a Shirley Temple doll. During my teen and college years, Shirley was almost forgotten, but my interest was renewed when I was returning from a vacation one summer and we stopped at an antique shop. There, sitting on a shelf in only her underclothes, was a 13 inch composition Shirley. Memories surfaced and I was a child again in the mountains of West Virginia. I found that after all these years, I still wanted a Shirley Temple doll. I bought the doll and she looked at me through crazed eyes and I thought she was beautiful. I only intended to buy one doll, but since that time I have added many Shirley dolls to my collection. I believe my most prized possession is the first truly mint-in-box Shirley I found to purchase. She is 18 inches tall, complete with the photograph included in the box. Even the box is factory mint. I guess she represents to me, the Shirley that I longed for in the 1930s. A dream finally realized after about forty-five years!"

Rosemary's childhood dream of owning a Shirley Temple doll was a dream that was shared by millions of other little girls throughout the 1930s, and her personal story is similar in many ways to so many other stories that collectors have shared with me while researching and gathering photographs for this project. So, here's to finding that doll or toy that you have always dreamed of owning. Here's to "the young at heart" and to proving that "it's never too late to have a happy childhood."

I sincerely hope that Shirley Temple collectors everywhere, both young and old, enjoy the information and illustrations that I have compiled throughout the following pages, as much as I have enjoyed putting them all together. Happy collecting!

Chapter 1

A Brief History

Rushed to stores just in time for Christmas, production of the first Shirley Temple doll began in the late fall of 1934 by the Ideal Novelty and Toy Company of Brooklyn, New York. Under the supervision of Abe Katz, head of manufacturing, and Mary Maidenbauer, vice president of doll production, Ideal quickly found itself unable to keep up with the overwhelming flood of orders coming in from all across the country, and production was almost immediately three weeks behind schedule. It seemed that the world's most famous child star was now well on her way to becoming the world's most famous doll as well.

For the children of the 1930s, who sat mesmerized in the nation's countless darkened movie theaters entranced by Shirley's singing and dancing, there was now a wonderful way to take their favorite little star home with them, in the form of a beautiful poseable doll. Absolutely every little girl simply had to have one for her very own. In an effort to meet public demand for the doll, Ideal increased its employees by nearly 50% and eventually acquired the services of several additional companies to help make wigs and clothing. Before long, production was again back on schedule and department stores throughout the country were soon busy stocking their shelves with "The World's Darling," the "genuine" Shirley Temple doll.

20″ Composition. All original from *The Blue Bird* (1939.) *Rita Dubas Collection.*

8

In late 1934, a kind of "Shirley Temple fever" began sweeping the nation. Moviegoers had become totally captivated with the dimpled child wonder and soon, nearly every motion picture studio in Hollywood was frantically searching to find their own child star sensation. Published nationwide, bold casting headlines declared, **"YOUR CHILD SHOULD BE IN THE MOVIES!"** Reading like an open invitation to fame, fortune and stardom, star-struck parents from every corner of the country quickly packed up their belongings, and with "Baby" in tow, they began heading west for the land of sunshine and opportunity.

Shirley Temple's tremendous success and popularity launched the beginning of a baby bread-winner hysteria on the film industry, that over the next five to ten years, as the phenomenon of the child star craze reached its peek, brought an estimated one thousand children a day pouring steadily into the studios and streets of Hollywood. Of those children, those who would earn even a single week's expenses in one entire year from work in the movies was less than one in fifteen thousand. This harsh realization eventually sent most disillusioned families back home within two or three fantasy-shattered months. Hollywood gossip columnist Hedda Hopper wrote of the times, "I used to wonder if there wasn't a special sub-human species of womankind that bred children for the sole purpose of dragging them to Hollywood."

Throughout the 1930s, Shirley Temple singlehandedly symbolized the name Hollywood. For moviegoers seeking refuge or a means of escape from the continuing burdens and realities of the nation's great depression, her motion pictures provided a magical, innocent place. For the fifteen cent price of admission, dreams would come true, and with a smile and a song, absolutely anything was possible. Shirley was instantly catapulted into the center stage spotlight of Hollywood's magical world following her first big break in the Fox Film Corporation production of *Stand Up And Cheer* in 1934. Wearing a red and white polka-dot dress, she was featured in a musical number titled "Baby Take A Bow." The adorable song and dance routine delighted audiences worldwide, and her cameo performance was the highlight of the entire film. Taking her final bow at the film's conclusion, Shirley was now and forever, a star.

Shirley's Early Life

Shirley Temple's journey to stardom began some twelve miles west of the bright lights of Hollywood, in the small seashore community of Santa Monica, California. It was here that her parents, George and Gertrude Temple, lived an average quiet life with their two sons George Jr. and Jack. All of that would change however, in the summer of 1927, when Gertrude suddenly decided to turn the entire family and their peaceful existence, upside-down.

It all started when Gertrude's two closest friends each gave birth to a beautiful baby girl with sweet little wisps of blond curly hair on top of their heads. Gertrude had always wanted a little girl of her own and she was determined, now more than ever, not to be left out. She boldly announced to her husband George, that she intended to have another baby, or else!

Before long, Gertrude's prayers were answered when she learned the news that she was indeed expecting another child. Her strong self-determination would not end there however. Being pregnant again was simply not enough; she wanted a baby girl. She immediately picked out the name Shirley Jane and set out on a personal crusade to completely fill her life with beautiful thoughts, sights and sounds. Bathing herself in bright feminine colors and scents, she began reading poetry and listening to sweet melodic music on the radio. Taking long walks along the shore, she would often stop to smell wild flowers or to watch children at play. She felt certain that she could somehow imprint these feminine images onto her unborn child and the dream of having a baby girl would come true.

Shirley Jane Temple was born at 9 p.m. on April 23, 1928. Gertrude had gotten her wish—a beautiful brown-eyed baby girl, complete with a dimple in each cheek. Born completely bald, there were no little wisps of blond curly hair as there were on her friend's babies, but that didn't seem to matter. It was clearly love at first sight, and quite obvious to everyone that the two were now totally inseparable.

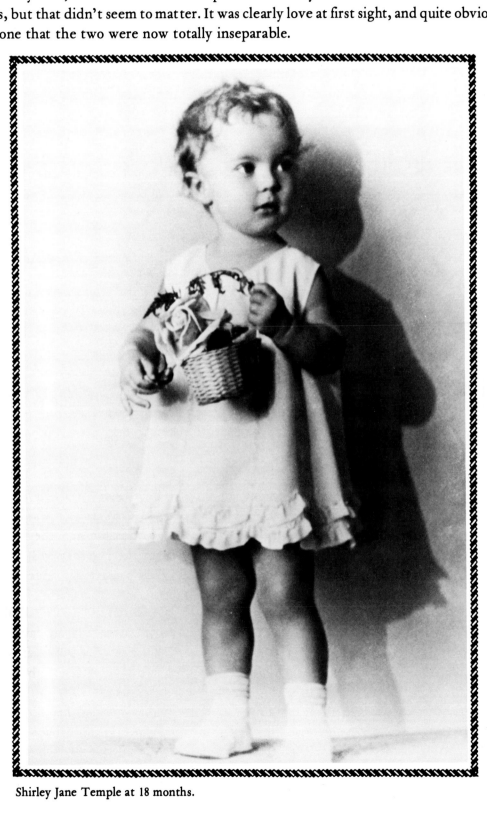

Shirley Jane Temple at 18 months.

As the months quickly passed, the Temple house was now constantly filled with music and dancing, as Gertrude continued her prenatal campaign of filling her little girl's life with a total artistic endowment. Almost immediately, sensing an inborn aptitude towards rhythm and music, she enrolled Shirley in Ethel Meglin's Dance Studio in Hollywood.

Though barely three years old, the newest "Meglin Kiddie" showed immediate promise. She was an outstanding, attentive student who learned quickly. With a sharp memory for routines, she excelled at nearly everything put before her and simply loved every single minute. At fifty cents a lesson, she was first taught a time-step and a soft shoe. Later, with sand sprinkled on the floor, she learned how to strut and how to make a "big exit," with a shuffle-off-to-Buffalo. Next came the buck-and-wing, clog, tango, Charleston, waltz, rumba, and even a little ballet.

A motion picture producer from Educational Films named Jack Hays, along with his partner, director Charles Lamont, stopped by the Meglin Studios one day looking for several children for a series of comedy film shorts they were planning called *Baby Burlesks*. They carefully scrutinized Mrs. Meglin's current crop of "Meglin Kiddies," proudly billed as "Kute, Klever and Kunning," without much interest. Then they spotted Shirley hiding under the piano, refusing to come out. They pointed to Shirley, with her adorable frowning eyebrows and pouting out-thrusted lower lip, and shouted, "We want her!"

Produced in 1931, the first *Baby Burlesk* was a spoof on the hit picture *The Front Page,* titled *The Runt Page.* The film fizzled-out quickly at the box office as an exploitive venture of rather questionable taste and production quality. Shirley appeared on screen, along with the other cast members, dressed in adult looking clothing from the waist up, but from the waist down, they each wore a large diaper fastened with a giant safety pin. It was not a very impressive debut for Shirley, but her salary of $10 a day was nothing to walk away from, not to mention Gertrude's retainer of $5 per week as hairdresser and seamstress. The Temple's signed a two year contract with Educational Films, crossed their fingers and hoped for the best.

War Babies (1932). The second of eight films in the *Baby Burlesk* series.

The official signing of Shirley's studio contract with
the Fox Film Corporation. Pictured are parents
Gertrude and George Temple. Summer 1934.

Baby Burlesks continued, in spite of their first failure, and these films included; *War Babies, The Pie Covered Wagon, Glad Rags To Riches, The Kid's Last Fight, Kid In Hollywood, Pollytix In Washington* and *Kid In Africa,* all produced in 1932. Following *Baby Burlesks,* Shirley appeared in five more comedies for Educational Films, the most successful of which were, *Merrily Yours* and *Dora's Dunking Doughnuts,* in 1933. Then, on a loan-out basis, she appeared in small, mostly unnoticeable roles in films for Tower Productions, Universal Pictures, Paramount, Fox Film Corporation, First National Pictures and Warner Brothers. This ended on September 28, 1933, when Jack Hays and Educational Films filed for bankruptcy. George Temple bought-out the remainder of his daughter's existing contract for $25 in cash and for awhile, the tiny movie veteran's future seemed rather uncertain. Less than one year later however, Shirley was at Fox Studios making *Stand Up And Cheer,* the film that would instantly make her a star and establish her as "The World's Darling."

Ideal Novelty and Toy Company

Realizing the tremendous money-making potential in Hollywood's newest little star, the Ideal Novelty and Toy Company quickly obtained an exclusive copyright to manufacture a doll, using Shirley's name and likeness. The original idea of manufacturing a Shirley Temple doll was brought to Ideal nearly a year earlier however, by a leading doll clothing designer named Mollye Goldman. Mollye had spotted Shirley in the film *Merrily Yours* and was certain that she was somehow destined for stardom. Following the great success of *Stand Up And Cheer,* production arrangements were immediately set into motion, and by Christmastime, thousands of lucky little girls from all across the country each had a beautiful Shirley Temple doll, bearing a tremendous likeness to the tiny dimpled starlet.

The Shirley Temple doll was first sculpted out of wax by master doll artist Bernard Lipfert. The wax designs were carefully made into molds which were then filled with a special wood pulp material called "composition." The six piece all-composition dolls are jointed at the neck, arms and legs, and are marked on the back of the head and/or the body. These markings varied from year to year during production and from size to size. With raised lettering, most of the dolls are marked "SHIRLEY TEMPLE/IDEAL NOV. & TOY CO." on the back of their head and "SHIRLEY TEMPLE," on the body. Additionally, some of the earliest dolls are marked only on the head and some of the later bodies also feature a number indicating their size.

Within one year of production, the dolls were available in a total of nine sizes including; 11 inch(28cm), 13 inch(33cm), 16 inch(41cm), 17 inch(43cm), 18 inch(46cm), 20 inch(51cm), 22 inch(56cm), 25 inch (64cm) and the largest size at 27 inch(69cm). A word is necessary here regarding composition doll sizes. Measuring from the tip of the toe, to the top of the head, a doll's actual height quite often will vary up to one inch either way from its mold size, due to an expansion or shrinkage factor of composition at the time of production. Many of these dolls will include a "+" or "-" marking on the back to indicate such a variation. For example, a 22 inch doll actually measuring 23 inches in height might be marked on the back, "SHIRLEY TEMPLE/22+."

Shirley Temple dolls have sleep eyes made of glass in colors of hazel, green or blue which close when the doll is reclined. The eyes feature real upper lashes with hand painted lower lashes, eyebrows, nostrils and lips. There is a light blush painted to cheeks, wrists and knees, and a dimple in each cheek. They have an open mouth, six teeth and a metal or felt tongue.

Wigs for the dolls were made exclusively of mohair, with large, sausage-style curls all around the head. Color shades ranged from light to golden blond. Each wig features a silk ribbon tied into a small bow on the top of the head, in several outfit matching colors.

Composition facial moldings of the "genuine" Shirley Temple doll, as designed by Bernard Lipfert. Pictured are 16", 18", 20" and 22" dolls.

The very first Shirley Temple dolls wore an exact copy of Shirley's red and white polka-dotted dancing dress from the film *Stand Up And Cheer*. The outfit was also available with blue or green polka-dots. Then, beginning in 1935, an unlimited number of other outfits, each in several different colors and fabric design, were made available for the dolls. Most of these outfits were replicas of the costumes Shirley wore in her motion pictures. From 1934 through 1936, these outfits were designed exclusively by Mollye Goldman. The dolls also wore combination slip/undies made of organdy, trimmed with lace, white rayon socks and imitation leather shoes, most often in white or black with a center snap or tie, and a silver metal buckle fastened over the toe. Shoes and socks varied slightly with each of the different outfits and from size to size.

20″ All original from *Stand Up And Cheer* (1934). This is an excellent example of the first Shirley Temple doll manufactured by Ideal. Doll is marked only on the back of the head, "IDEAL N & T CO." Fully jointed on a six-piece, all composition body. Golden blond mohair wig in original set. Hazel sleep eyes made of glass, with real upper lashes, painted lower lashes, eyebrows and lips. Open smiling mouth with six teeth and a felt tongue. Pronounced dimples. Doll is wearing red and white coin-dotted organdy dress with red trim and a red silk ribbon tied just above the waist. Woven "NRA" cotton dress tag, original pin. Doll is shown with original price tag attached to the hem of her dress. Tag reads "STRAWBRIDGE & CLOTHIER/$5.95."

The earliest Shirley Temple doll outfits each have a woven cotton dress tag, usually attached at the back, which reads, "SHIRLEY TEMPLE/ DOLL DRESS/REG. U.S. PAT. OFF./IDEAL NOV. & TOY CO.." At the end of each tag, there is an emblem of a blue eagle, along with the initials "N R A." The initials stand for the National Recovery Administration, which was a federal legislative agency briefly enacted in the early days of President Franklin D. Roosevelt's "New Deal." The N.R.A. was developed as a means of helping to increase the nation's employment rate. The agency was dissolved completely by January of 1936 and Ideal (having already switched to rayon tags), issued new clothing tags in late 1935. Without the blue eagle and N.R.A. initials, these tags read, "Genuine/SHIRLEY TEMPLE/DOLL/REGISTERED U.S. PAT. OFF./IDEAL NOV. & TOY CO./MADE IN U.S.A." Combination slip/undies are tagged only to indicate size.

Baby Shirley Doll

By late 1935, Ideal also introduced the Baby Shirley Temple doll. With a chubby, toddler-style body, the dolls have molded painted hair or a curly mohair wig glued over the molded hair. They feature a composition head, arms and legs on a stuffed cloth body, complete with a crier mechanism sewn inside the chest. Some of the later Baby Shirley Temple dolls featured hard rubber arms as well, but these were marketed only on a limited basis. Additionally, many Shirley Temple dolls were featuring "flirty" or "magic" eyes, which moved from side to side when the doll's head was tilted or turned.

Each Shirley Temple doll came in a fully labeled gift box, along with an 8" x 10" photograph of Shirley and later dolls included hair curlers in each box, to help keep their hair waved and curled. Attached to the clothing, each doll wears a pink or tan celluloid pin which reads, "THE WORLD'S DARLING/GENUINE SHIRLEY TEMPLE AN IDEAL DOLL" or "THE WORLD'S DARLING/GENUINE SHIRLEY TEMPLE DOLL." Two separate photographs of Shirley were used in the center of three original pin styles. The outer edge of each pin reads, "IDEAL NOVELTY AND TOY CO./ MADE IN U.S.A. REG. U.S. PAT. OFF. HER SIGNATURE." The pins were manufactured for Ideal by The Whitehead & Hoag Company of Newark, New Jersey and Cellomet Products Co. of New York City.

By late 1940, the public's investment in Shirley Temple dolls reached an estimated $45 million in total sales receipts, making her at the time, the single most successful doll or toy ever produced. The enormous success of the dolls quickly led to an endless supply of all sorts of other Shirley Temple items (manufactured by a number of different companies), each in conjunction with the release of her latest film. These items included; Shirley Temple hair ribbons, head bands, hats, shoes, socks, slippers, overcoats, dresses, handkerchiefs, purses, soap, dishes, sheet music, sewing kits, hair curlers, pocket mirrors, writing tablets, stationary, fountain pens, pencil boxes, playing cards, string holders, fans, pins, badges, anklets, bracelets, charms, rings, barrettes, candy, chocolates, paint sets, coloring books, storybooks, movie related books, doll buggies, post cards and photographs. All of these items sold with remarkable success, and Shirley Temple herself was soon nothing short of a national obsession.

Original dress tags for the composition Shirley Temple doll. Top: Woven cotton "NRA" tag. Middle: Rayon "NRA" tag. Bottom: Rayon tag. One of these tags appeared on all "genuine" Shirley Temple doll outfits and can be found sewn in the front, back, side, or inside of each garment.

Combination slip/undies made of organdy. Tagged "16".

18" all original Shirley Temple Baby by Ideal. Molded painted hair, flirty eyes. Outfit is pink organdy with silk ribbons. Rayon "NRA" dress tag, original pin. Chubby toddler body features dimples in cheeks, back of hands and on the knees. *Lorna Erb Collection.*

18

This 11″ all original doll, dressed in pink organdy from *Curly Top* (1935), managed to leave the factory in a standard Ideal box. Very unusual and extremely rare. *Rita Dubas Collection.*

Three versions of the original box labels designed for the composition dolls. Each box contained a heavy cardboard neck-rest and leg-stay, and each doll was wrapped in white or pink tissue paper.

Three original pin styles designed for the composition Shirley Temple doll.

SHIRLEY TEMPLE

Autographed 8" x 10" give-away photo which accompanied all of the composition dolls and outfits, boxed and sold separately.

In an effort to jump on the lucrative Shirley Temple bandwagon, several unauthorized doll companies soon began making their own versions of the Shirley Temple doll, using any means possible to try and outsmart Ideal's sole copyright. Unable to use Shirley's name in any way, these dolls appeared on toy store shelves right next to the "genuine" articles, each with their own catchy name to try and catch the public's eye and remind them of Shirley. Most often selling at a cheaper, more affordable price, names like; Bright Star, Miss Charming, Little Miss Movie and The Movie Queen, were some of the more successful imitations.

For the most part, these "imitation Shirley's" are easy to recognize. First, they are usually unmarked and never say "SHIRLEY TEMPLE" on their heads, bodies, or original clothing. Their mohair wigs quite often are close to Ideal's design and construction, but their facial moldings greatly lack Bernard Lipfert's original detailed sculpturing and expression. Also, most of these dolls feature eyes made of tin, as opposed to Ideal's (usual) glass eyes. Throughout the 1930s, Ideal manufactured "Genuine SHIRLEY TEMPLE DOLL OUTFITS," sold separately from the dolls, in all sizes. Many of these tagged outfits can now be found, some fifty years later, dressed on these Shirley look-alikes, only adding to the confusion as to whether or not the doll is the "genuine" article. Additionally, there were

13″ imitation Shirley Temple as *The Little Colonel*, manufactured by the Alexander Doll Company, of New York, N.Y.

13″ Shirley Temple by Ideal. All original from *The Little Colonel* (1934). Note the differences in expression, facial molding, wig construction and clothing design, from the imitation made by Alexander.

Full-length view for comparison of the "genuine" Ideal Shirley Temple doll and the Alexander version.

Original boxed outfit for an 18″ doll. Dress is made of yellow and brown dimity, from *The Littlest Rebel* (1935). Note the original hanger, pin and rayon dress tag. Box also contains the original sales receipt for 98 cents plus 2 cents tax, from *Macy's* department store, New York, N.Y.

8" unlicensed Shirley Temple doll made in Japan. Doll is all composition and all original as shown. Pictured with its original box. Body and underwear are marked "JAPAN."

18" unlicensed all cloth Shirley Temple doll. Clothing appears to be from *The Little Colonel* and is tagged, "Blossom Doll Company/N.Y. N.Y."

several other unlicensed Shirley Temple dolls, including a mechanical doll playing a pipe organ, a dancing doll who does a jig, a miniature composition doll from Japan, and a series of foreign and domestic cloth dolls.

Shirley Temple's mother, Mrs. Gertrude Temple, had always taught her daughter to "sparkle" whenever she was in front of a camera, and Shirley sparkled indeed throughout her entire film career. Spanning a period of eighteen years, her films included, among many others, major hits such as; *Little Miss Marker* (1934), *Baby Take A Bow* (1934), *Bright Eyes* (1934), *The Little Colonel* (1934), *Curly Top* (1935), *The Littlest Rebel* (1935), *Captain January* (1936), *Poor Little Rich Girl* (1936), *Wee Willie Winkie* (1937) and *Heidi* (1937). Shirley also introduced moviegoers to many delightful songs such as; "Baby Take A Bow," "On The Good Ship Lollipop" and "Animal Crackers In My Soup." Her most memorable screen moments were spent dancing side by side with Bill "Bojangles" Robinson however, and together they literally made film history as they masterfully tap danced their way through four motion pictures, *The Little Colonel* and *The Littlest Rebel* in 1934 and 1935, followed by *Rebecca Of Sunnybrook Farm* and *Just Around The Corner* in 1938.

The Ideal Novelty and Toy Company always kept right in step with Shirley's film career, and throughout production, they continually introduced their Shirley Temple dolls wearing outfits patterned directly from her latest movie costumes. Today, many of these outfits are much sought after by serious collectors as their original availability was issued on a rather limited time frame, now making them extremely rare. These include; the aviator costume from *Bright Eyes*, *The Little Colonel*, *Wee Willie Winkie*, *Heidi*, the Texas Ranger/Cowgirl and *The Blue Bird*. These outfits were also made in fewer sizes, most likely due to the amount of detail in their design and construction.

Beginning sometime in early 1936, a new facial mold was designed for the Shirley Temple doll which better represented the growing and changing young star. Replacing the original molds, many of which had become extremely worn from extended usage and time, these new dolls featured a rounder, fuller looking face with a lighter complexion, dark eye shadow, more defined eyebrows and lower painted lashes, higher coloring to cheeks, wrists and knees. A new wig design was also introduced which came parted down the center and was framed with small pin curls.

Close-up showing the beautiful facial sculpturing of the original 18″ composition doll mold. Note the original mohair wig in its original set, clear hazel eyes, painted eyebrows, lower lashes and lips, plus the unmistakable Shirley Temple dimples. Outfit is from *Curly Top* (1935).

This close-up photograph illustrates the updated 1936, 18″ facial molding. Note the higher forehead, lighter complexion, dark eye shadow and more defined painted features. Also, mohair wig is now parted down the center. Outfit is from *Curly Top*.

Without question, Shirley Temple's famous golden blond curls were her signature trademark. They were created originally, strictly out of necessity, to help thwart a tendency towards frizziness caused by humidity. Each evening following supper, Mrs. Temple carved the corner of a large bar of *Castile* soap into thin shavings and then melted them in a small pan on top of the stove. Applying the warm gooey paste to her daughter's scalp, a vigorous scrubbing was followed by an eye-stinging vinegar rinse and the rolling of fifty-six unvarying tight little curls. Each night, Mrs. Gertrude Temple fashioned an unmistakable trademark of curls which eventually made her child the single most recognizable image in motion picture history, with the exception perhaps of Charlie Chaplin or Mickey Mouse.

As the quintessential child star of the 1930s, Shirley Temple reflected a persona of the perfect child. She instantly came to represent the model for the child every parent wanted and every child wanted to be. Rising out of the depression years, her films broke nearly every ticket sales record, topping even those of Hollywood's king, Clark Gable. She was presented a special miniature Oscar at the Seventh Annual Academy Awards Ceremony for "grateful recognition of her outstanding contribution to screen entertainment during the year 1934," and the motion picture industry proclaimed her to be its "Top Box Office Star" for the years 1935, 1936, 1937 and 1938, an unprecedented and never equaled four straight years. Even President Franklin D. Roosevelt issued a statement regarding Shirley which read; "It's a splendid thing that for just fifteen cents an American can go to a movie and look at the smiling face of a baby and forget his troubles. As long as we have Shirley Temple, we will be alright."

Seeing an original Shirley Temple doll again, or even for the very first time, you feel as if you can almost hear Shirley singing "On The Good Ship Lollipop" or "Animal Crackers In My Soup." Even the most hardened or advanced collector can't help but stare in amazement at the child star doll who so keenly reflects a time so nostalgic and innocent. One marvels at the original craftsmanship and attention to detail, with every lock of hair so meticulously placed. Fifty-eight years after the doll was first introduced, she now stands so regal and symbolic of her era. She seems to represent so much more than was originally intended, so much more than just a toy.

Vinyl Dolls

Production of the composition doll ended in 1939. New dolls, made this time out of vinyl, were issued by Ideal eighteen years later, in late 1957, in conjunction with the release of Shirley's motion pictures to television audiences, and the start of her own television series for NBC.

Shirley Temple's Storybook premiered on January 12, 1958, and the sixteen separate programs ran until December 21, 1958. With Shirley serving as narrator and hostess, the series featured adaptations of fairytales and classic children's stories including; *Tom and Huck, The Land Of OZ, Kim, Little Men, Beauty and the Beast, Rapunzel, The Sleeping Beauty, Cinderella, Rip van Winkle, Charlotte's Web, Son Of Aladdin, Rumpelstiltskin, Mother Goose* and *The Legend of Sleepy Hollow*. The new vinyl Shirley Temple dolls featured outfits fashioned from many of these children's storybook characters as well as authentic costumes from her early motion pictures.

Ranging in sizes from 12 inch(31cm) to 36 inch(91cm), these new dolls were manufactured with a vinyl head, rooted synthetic dark blond hair, and a hard plastic torso, arms and legs. Composition was no longer the medium of choice. The 1950s brought with it the age of

The 1957 vinyl Shirley Temple doll. Pictured from L. to R., *Heidi, Wee Willie Winkie, Rebecca Of Sunnybrook Farm, Captain January.* Dolls are marked on head "Ideal Doll/ST-12," body marked "ST-12-N." Clothing is tagged "Shirley Temple/made by IDEAL TOY CORP." These 12" dolls are shown with their original plastic script pins and wrist tags.

plastics, automation and mass production to the doll industry and the detailed craftsmanship of the past was soon all but forgotten. The modern Shirley Temple dolls no longer resembled tiny works of art, as did the original composition dolls. But the public didn't seem to mind this change in quality. Like the earlier dolls of the 1930s, toy buyers just couldn't seem to get enough. Within six months of production, Ideal sold over three hundred thousand vinyl Shirley Temple dolls. Other new Shirley Temple items were soon available including; storybooks, record albums, dishes, hats, coats, dresses, children's handbags, doll clothing patterns, coloring books, paper dolls, and even a magnetic TV theater.

Following its 100th Anniversary Celebration in 1972, the Montgomery Wards department store chain issued its own vinyl Shirley Temple doll, wearing two versions of the red and white polka-dotted dress from *Stand Up And Cheer.* This doll was available in one size of 15 inches(38cm).

In 1973, Ideal issued another vinyl Shirley using a new mold and facial design. This 16 inch(41cm) doll was available in four separate outfits including; *The Little Colonel, Captain January, Rebecca Of Sunnybrook Farm* and *Stand Up And Cheer.* All of the vinyl dolls are fully jointed on a six-piece body with rooted synthetic hair.

16" vinyl Shirley Temple from *Stand Up And Cheer.* Shown with original picture box. Doll is marked on head "1972/Ideal Toy Corp./ST-14-H-312/Hong Kong," body marked "Ideal/1972/2M-5634/1."

15" all original vinyl Shirley Temple. Produced in 1972 for *Montgomery Wards.* Marked on head "Hong Kong/Ideal Doll/St-15-N," body marked "Ideal St-15/Hong Kong." Dress is tagged "Made in Hong Kong."

Catalogue tear sheet showing Ideal's 1982 vinyl Shirley Temple dolls.

The Shirley Temple Doll Collection Series

A

B

C

D

E

IDEAL

F

Shirley Temple Collection

...eal brings back "America's Sweet-...art" just as she was: with curls, ...nples and the sweet smile that was ...gic for children and adults. It's all ...re for today's little girls to love ...ain. The collection consists of six ...lls, each dressed in a fashion from a ...ssic movie role, inspired by Mrs. ...irley Temple Black's favorites. The ...gantly detailed outfits and finely ...ulpted features combine to give you ...rue collectible. Each doll has lashed ...es, luxurious hair, fully poseable. ...8" and 12" sizes. Vinyl.

Heidi
...200-2....8"............$24.00
...200-8...12"............$38.00

B. Stowaway
53200-6.....8"..............$24.00
53200-12....12"..............$38.00

C. Stand Up and Cheer
53200-1....8"..............$24.00
53200-7...12"..............$38.00

D. The Little Colonel
53200-5.....8"..............$24.00
53200-11...12"..............$38.00

E. Captain January
53200-3....8"..............$24.00
53200-9...12"..............$38.00

F. The Littlest Rebel
53200-4.....8"..............$24.00
53200-10...12"..............$38.00

7

Designed by Elke Hutchens, the most recent Shirley Temple doll is made of porcelain by The Danbury Mint. Doll measures 20″ tall and is all original from *The Little Princess* (1939). Using the same mold, a series of four dolls were issued beginning in 1990. Other costumes include; *Bright Eyes, Curly Top* and *Dimples*. Marked on the back of the neck "Shirley Temple/ 1990 MBI."

Shirley Temple dolls are still being manufactured today, most recently made of porcelain by the Danbury Mint of Norwalk, Connecticut. However, the original composition dolls made by Ideal from 1934 to 1939, will always remain the true treasures. With their endless array of movie costumes, beautiful golden curls and expressive dimpled faces, the dolls instantly bring a flood of wonderful memories of Shirley and her delightful motion pictures rushing back into our hearts and minds. The dolls somehow touch the child in all of us and remind us of that innocent time long ago, when we once dreamed of Santa Claus and magical lands of adventure and make-believe. Time has now marched on, but the dolls remain, allowing us to imagine for a moment that little Shirley's uplifting spirit and sweet young face are with us once again, and are only a box of popcorn and a fifteen cent Saturday matinee away.

Research for this book included the viewing of every Shirley Temple film currently available on video tape. Extra care has been taken to CORRECTLY IDENTIFY the following costumes from the films in which they actually appeared.

On the verge of stardom, circa 1933.

Shirley poses with an early 22″ prototype Shirley Temple doll. This photograph was part of the advanced 1934 marketing campaign released several months prior to the sale of the doll. Outfit and facial molding as shown, were modified before actual production of the dolls began.

Wearing matching cotton sailboat dresses, Shirley poses again with the prototype doll. This outfit was eventually manufactured and sold as a part of Ideal's Shirley Temple doll clothing line, with slight variations from the outfit shown.

11" all original from *Stand Up And Cheer* (1934). Wearing coin-dotted organdy dress with a silk ribbon tied at the waist. Rayon dress tag, original pin. Outfit was available in red, blue, or green. Marked "SHIRLEY TEMPLE" on head and body.

Chapter 2

Shirley Temple Dolls and Fashions

It would be nearly impossible to catalogue every single Shirley Temple doll outfit ever made, as their total number seems almost infinite, each with many variations in design, fabric and color. The following illustrations however, will provide the collector with a well-rounded view as to what was originally available for "The World's Darling," the "genuine" Shirley Temple doll.

Composition Dolls

1934-1939

13″ all original from *Stand Up And Cheer* (1934). This organdy dress is a green version of the outfit previously shown. Woven "NRA" dress tag, original pin. Doll is pictured in original trunk along with two tagged outfits.

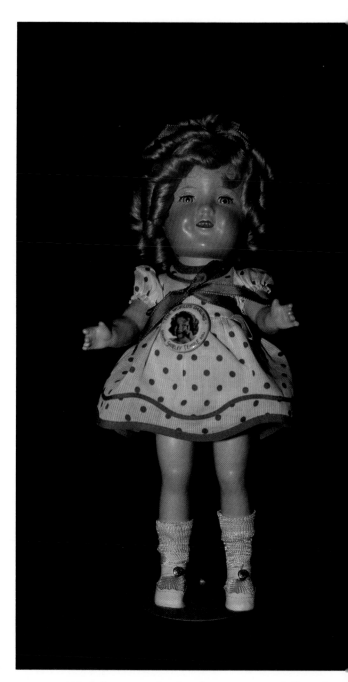

11" pristine mint condition, in original box. All original from *Stand Up And Cheer*. Marked on head "ll/SHIRLEY TEMPLE," body marked "SHIRLEY TEMPLE/ll." Wearing dimity dress with solid blue polka-dots printed in fabric, trimmed with a silk ribbon tied at the waist. Rayon dress tag, original pin. Note the original give-away photograph behind the doll and the cardboard stays used to hold the doll in place for shipping.

11" doll as previously shown, removed from her original box. A highly unusual feature on this doll is her eyes made out of tin. Nearly all composition Shirley Temple dolls are found with glass eyes. The 11" size seems to be the only exception to this rule. When identifying and comparing, slight variations can almost always be expected on both the dolls and the doll fashions. With increasing orders to be filled and deadlines to meet, revisions and substitutions were made as needed throughout all stages of production. Consistency can always be found however, in overall quality.

"The World's Darling" as she appeared in *Stand Up And Cheer* (1934).

Variation of the polka-dot dancing dress from *Stand Up And Cheer*, circa 1935. Made of organdy and shown with matching hat and sunsuit. Rayon dress tag. This outfit was also available in blue and was often sold as part of the trunk wardrobe.

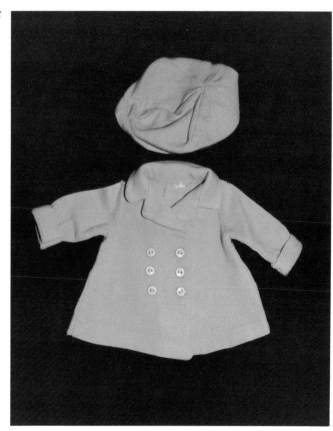

Wool coat and hat from *Little Miss Marker* (1934). Fits 18″ doll. Woven "NRA" tag has been removed. *Lorna Erb Collection.*

From *Bright Eyes* (1934). Made of cotton, this pleated dress fits a 16″ doll and was available in several colors and plaid variations. "NRA" dress tag.

13″ all original from *Bright Eyes*. Note the redesigned 1936 facial molding with lighter complexion and dark eye shadow. Also note plaid variation from previous photograph. Most of the later edition composition dolls featured redesigned, vented imitation leather shoes as shown. Rayon dress tag, original pin. Doll is marked on head "13/SHIRLEY TEMPLE," body marked "USA/13."

Shirley's plaid dress from *Bright Eyes*, was worn while
singing her signature trademark song "On The Good
Ship Lollipop."

Shirley models her aviator film costume from *Bright
Eyes*.

Close-up of aviator outfit showing jacket and facial
detailing.

22″ all original aviator outfit from *Bright Eyes* (1934). Red leather jacket with blue cotton pants. Original pin. Marked "SHIRLEY TEMPLE" on head and body.

Pictured with original box, this corduroy coat and hat are from the final scene of *Bright Eyes*. Woven "NRA" tag, original pin. Fits 16″ doll.

Beginning in 1934, this pleated organdy costume was used in many publicity photographs promoting several of Shirley's early motion pictures. It became one of the first outfits available for the composition doll as well.

18" all original, circa 1934. Wearing knife-pleated, pale green organdy dress featuring punched embroidered collar and a pink silk ribbon. Woven "NRA" dress tag, original pin. Marked on head "IDEAL N & T CO.," body marked "SHIRLEY TEMPLE." This outfit was also available in pink or blue.

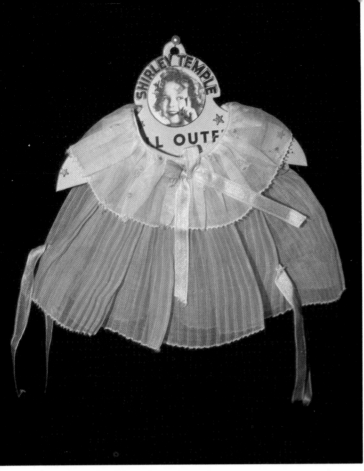

Light blue example of the organdy dress previously shown. Rayon "NRA" dress tag. Fits 16" doll. Shown with original cardboard hanger which came with all outfits sold separately from the doll.

18" all original, in very early 1934 outfit. Made of light pink organdy. Collar features pink hemstitching and dress has wider ironed-in pleats than previously shown. Silk ribbons tie at the wrists for posing. Woven "NRA" dress tag, original pin. Marked on head "SHIRLEY TEMPLE/COP. IDEAL/N & T CO.," body marked "SHIRLEY TEMPLE."

18" all original doll wearing a slight variation of the outfit previously shown. Very early doll, 1934.

42

Doll from previous photo wearing original velveteen coat and hat.

This outfit was pictured in many publicity photos, including early promotions for *Baby Take A Baby* (1934). Made of cotton with silk ribbons. Woven "NRA" dress tag. Fits 16" doll. Also available in blue.

Opposite:

18" all original with original wardrobe trunk from *The Little Colonel* (1934). Wearing pink organdy dress with attached slip, trimmed with lace. Dress features tiny silk rose buds in yellow, green and blue. Original bonnet and plume, white pantaloons trimmed with two rows of lace. Original pin. Outfit was also available in green, lavender or blue. Blue silk ribbons as shown are not original. Marked on head "IDEAL N & T CO.," body marked "SHIRLEY TEMPLE/18."

20" heavy cardboard steamer trunk for an 18" doll. Features a leather strap-handle and corner guards, glued-on labels promoting Shirley's motion pictures, and a metal latch with a lock and key. Inside there are four cardboard hangers and two drawers. Wardrobe trunks were available in cardboard or wood for 13", 16" and 18" dolls.

Shirley poses in publicity outfit for *Baby Take A Bow* (1934).

13" all original from *The Little Colonel* (1934). Made of light blue organdy, this version has slight variations from the 18" doll previously shown. Many of the smaller *Little Colonel* dolls came without the bonnet as pictured. Note how the wrists can be fitted through small elastic loops for posing. Woven "NRA" dress tag, original pin. Head marked "SHIRLEY TEMPLE," body marked "SHIRLEY TEMPLE/13." Doll has her original box with $2.98 price tag.

13″ all original taffeta version of *The Little Colonel* outfit. Note the variations in design of collar, ruffles and pantaloons from the 13″ organdy outfit. Marked on head "SHIRLEY TEMPLE," body marked "SHIRLEY TEMPLE/13."

20″ all original blue organdy from *The Little Colonel*. Woven "NRA" dress tag, original pin. Doll is pictured alongside 20″ *Steiff* rabbit. Marked on head "SHIRLEY TEMPLE/IDEAL/ COP. N & T CO.," body marked "SHIRLEY TEMPLE."

13″ and 20″ all original dolls from *The Little Colonel*. Note variations in pantaloons, bonnets and shoes.

Shirley poses with a 27" doll in matching taffeta *Little Colonel* outfits.

This is an example of the largest size composition Shirley Temple doll at 27". All original pink taffeta from *The Little Colonel*. Woven "NRA" dress tag, original pin. Marked "SHIRLEY TEMPLE" on head and body. *Lorna Erb Collection.*

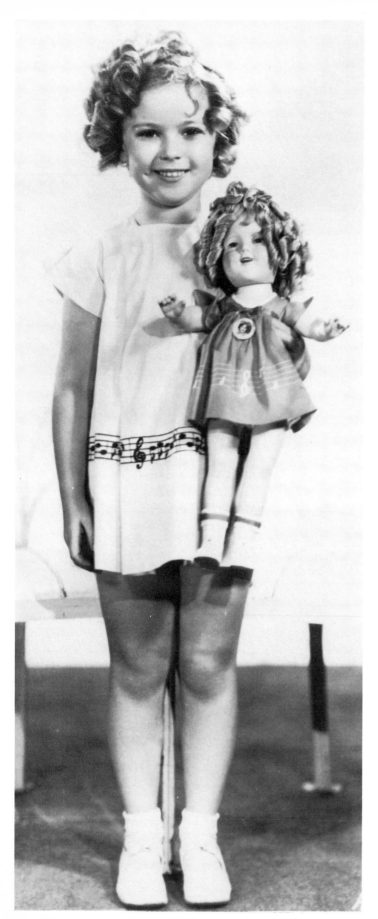

Shirley poses with a 22" doll in matching outfits from
Our Little Girl (1935).

16" outfit from *Our Little Girl* (1935). Red dimity dress
features glued-on treble clef and music note appliques.
Very rare to find this outfit with a matching hat.
Streamers tie at the back into a bow. Woven "NRA"
dress tag. Also available in blue.

From *Our Little Girl* (1935), this 16" outfit is made of
pique with glued-on white cotton scotty dog appliques.
Woven "NRA" dress tag. Larger examples of this
dress feature a third scotty dog in the center, just
below the collar line. Also available in blue or white.

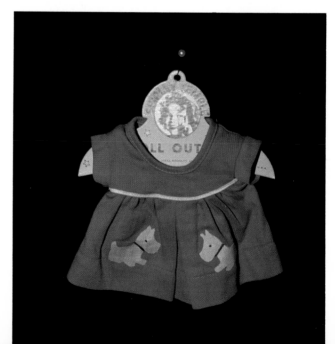

18" Version of the scotty dog dress from *Our Little Girl*. Note how the leash is attached to button.

Side view showing Rayon tag placement.

Shirley poses with a 22" doll in matching outfits from *Our Little Girl* (1935).

48

18" all original from *Curly Top* (1935). This knife-pleated, dotted swiss version of the *Curly Top* outfit is trimmed with blue silk ribbons and was also available in red or lavender. Note the variation on the socks. Rayon dress tag, original pin. Marked on head "18/SHIRLEY TEMPLE/COP. IDEAL N & T CO.," body marked "SHIRLEY TEMPLE/18-."

11" version of the *Curly Top* dotted swiss. Rayon dress tag, original pin. Marked on head "ll/SHIRLEY TEMPLE," body marked "SHIRLEY TEMPLE/ll."

Manufactured at the height of production, this 16" all original, mint-in-box doll is from *Curly Top* (1935). This is perhaps the most common outfit available for the composition doll. Outfit was made for all sizes, with many fabric variations and colors. Doll pictured is wearing knife-pleated, pink organdy with light blue ribbons on the collar, at the waist and tied at the wrists for posing. Rayon dress tag, original pin. Marked on head "16/SHIRLEY TEMPLE," body marked "SHIRLEY TEMPLE/16."

18″ all original, knife-pleated, star-burst version of the *Curly Top* outfit. Made of organdy, dress is aqua with brown stars and tiny pin-dots printed into the fabric. Rayon dress tag, original pin. Marked on head "18/SHIRLEY TEMPLE/COP. IDEAL/N & T CO.," body marked "18-."

Close-up showing the printed star-burst detailing. This outfit was also available in yellow or pink.

18″ all original, yellow star-burst design from *Curly Top* (1935). Rayon dress tag. Original pin. Marked "SHIRLEY TEMPLE" on head and body.

18″ all original from *Curly Top* (1935). Outfit is red pleated pique with embroidered flowers on bodice. Rayon dress tag, original pin. Marked on head "SHIRLEY TEMPLE," body marked "SHIRLEY TEMPLE/18."

18″ all original from *Curly Top* (1935), as previously shown. Doll is pictured wearing original white fur coat with a rayon dress tag. This outfit also came with a fur tam and muffler.

From *Curly Top* (1935), Shirley poses with 20″ doll in matching pleated, daisy dress. Outfit was available with tiny embroidered flowers and stitching or larger glued-on daisy appliques as shown.

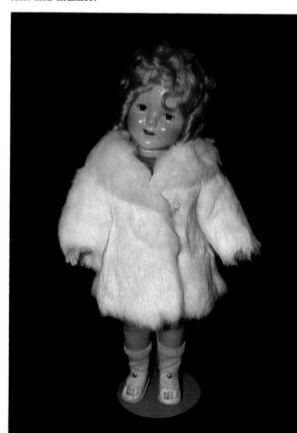

Striped cotton dress from *Curly Top* (1935). Rayon dress tag. Fits 20″ doll. Also available in blue and red. *Lorna Erb Collection.*

Shirley poses with 16″ doll in matching striped cotton dresses from *Curly Top* (1935).

20″ from *Curly Top* (1935). Outfit is black velvet with yellow taffeta. Bodice features floral embroidery and glued-on duck appliques. Rayon dress tag. This outfit was also available in green and yellow. Marked "SHIRLEY TEMPLE" on head and body. Shoes and socks have been replaced.

Curly Top (1935.)

Wicker doll buggy also manufactured by the F.A. Whitney Carriage Company, 1935.

Close-up showing the "Shirley Temple" hood knob and metal photo decal. Hubcaps are also labeled "Shirley Temple."

Shirley poses alongside a wooden Shirley Temple doll buggy, manufactured by the F.A. Whitney Carriage Company, of Leominster, Mass. Circa 1935. Two sizes were available in colors of black, blue, green, or grey. Also pictured is a 25″ all original Shirley Temple Baby doll.

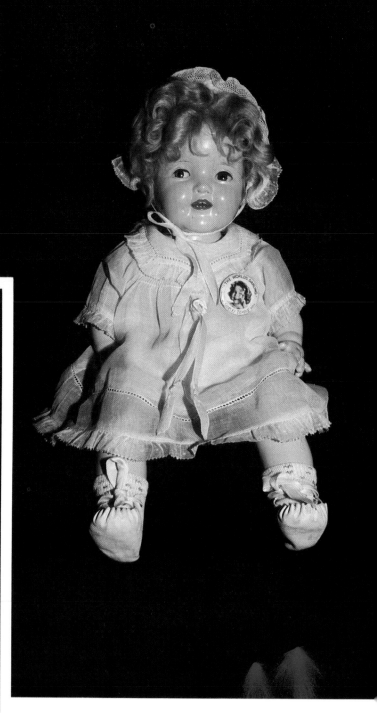

Opposite:
16″ all original Shirley Temple Baby. Features mohair wig and flirty eyes. Rayon dress tag, original pin. *Lorna Erb Collection.*

20″ all original Shirley Temple Baby. Rayon dress tag, original pin. Doll has composition head, arms and legs, on a stuffed cloth body. *Lorna Erb Collection.*

Dressed in her pleated dancing dress from *Curly Top*, Shirley poses with Ideal's 22″ Shirley Temple Baby.

56

This 16" doll is dressed in a pique, polka-dot outfit from *The Littlest Rebel* (1935). Shown with original organdy pantaloons, trimmed with two rows of lace. Grey felt hat is an exact copy of the original. Outfit was also available in yellow, and came without the pantaloons and hat as well. Rayon dress tag, original pin. Marked on head "SHIRLEY TEMPLE/60," body marked "SHIRLEY TEMPLE/16."

22" all original from *The Littlest Rebel* (1935). Wearing red and white, heavy cotton dress with organdy Peter Pan collar, organdy sleeves and pinafore. Rayon dress tag, original pin. Marked on head "SHIRLEY TEMPLE/COP. IDEAL N & T CO.," body marked "SHIRLEY TEMPLE/22-."

22" all original from *The Littlest Rebel* (1935). Wearing variation of the outfit previously shown. Note the slight differences such as collar trimmed with lace, rick-rack trim on sleeves, no pantaloons, shorter skirt length and patterned socks. Rayon dress tag, original pin. Marked "SHIRLEY TEMPLE" on head and body. *Marge Meisinger Collection.*

13" all original from *The Littlest Rebel* (1935). Yellow and brown version as previously shown. Rayon dress tag, original pin. Marked on head "13/SHIRLEY TEMPLE," body marked "SHIRLEY TEMPLE/13." Has original box with $3.00 price tag still attached.

Shirley Temple as *The Littlest Rebel* (1935).

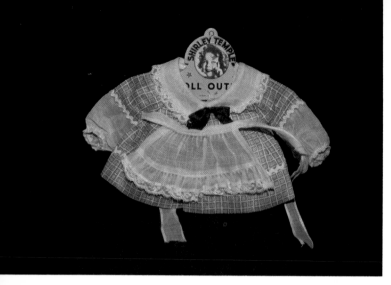

Another version of *The Littlest Rebel* outfit. Shown on original cardboard hanger. Fits 16″ doll.

18″ all original from *The Littlest Rebel* (1935). Made of cotton and organdy. In 1937, this outfit also appeared in magazine ads promoted as *Heidi*. Outfit was available in many colors and fabric designs, each with slight variations. Rayon dress tag, original pin. Marked on body "SHIRLEY TEMPLE."

22″ all original, dark blue version of the *Captain January* sailor suit. Note the white trim detailing. Rayon tag, original pin. Marked on head "SHIRLEY TEMPLE/COP. IDEAL/N & T CO.," body marked "SHIRLEY TEMPLE." *Marge Meisinger Collection.*

13″ all original from *Captain January* (1936). Marked on head "SHIRLEY TEMPLE," body marked "SHIRLEY TEMPLE/13."

18″ all original from *Captain January* (1936). Sailor suit is made of a medium weight, cotton twill fabric with glued-on anchor applique and red silk tie. Rayon tag, original pin. Marked on head "18/SHIRLEY TEMPLE/COP. IDEAL/N & T CO.," body marked "SHIRLEY TEMPLE/18."

Captain January (1936).

This black velveteen coat and hat was a special premium outfit fashioned expressly for Shirley's induction as an honorary member of The American Legion in 1935. Rayon "NRA" tag. Shown on 16″ doll.

20″ all original from *Captain January* (1936). Doll is wearing blue floral print, cotton school dress with ruffled organdy collar. Rayon dress tag, original pin. Marked on head "20/SHIRLEY TEMPLE/COP. IDEAL/N & T CO.," body marked "SHIRLEY TEMPLE 20★." Pictured with original purse, featuring a glued-on Shirley Temple cameo.

Another version of the *Captain January* school dress. The film version of this outfit also featured a matching bonnet. Doll is 13″ tall and all original. Rayon dress tag, original pin. Marked on head "SHIRLEY TEMPLE," body marked "SHIRLEY TEMPLE/13."

From *Captain January* (1936). Pleated pique, with silk ribbons. Rayon dress tag. Fits 16″ doll. Outfit was also available in red or green.

16″ all original from *Captain January* (1936). Green pique with silk ribbons. Rayon dress tag, original pin. Marked "SHIRLEY TEMPLE," on head and body. *Lorna Erb Collection.*

13" all original from *Poor Little Rich Girl* (1936). Sailor dress is pleated pique with white trim and a matching tam. Rayon dress tag, original pin. Outfit was also available in two shades of blue. Marked on head "SHIRLEY TEMPLE," body marked "SHIRLEY TEMPLE/13."

18" all original in original steamer trunk. Doll is wearing pique sunsuit with matching tam. Shown with matching sailor suit from *Poor Little Rich Girl*. Also pictured, original give-away photo and original pin. *Rita Dubas Collection.*

Blue version of the sailor dress from *Poor Little Rich Girl*, pictured with pique and organdy dress, circa 1935. Rayon "NRA" dress tag. Both of these outfits fit a 16" doll.

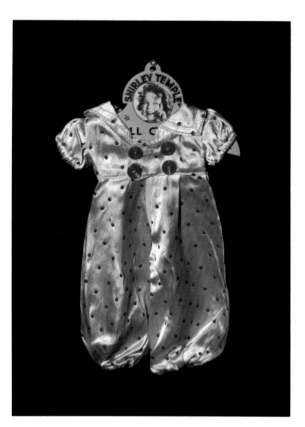

Silk pajamas from *Poor Little Rich Girl* (1936). Outfit features tiny flocked polka-dots and red plastic buttons. Rayon dress tag. Outfit is shown on original cardboard hanger. Fits 16" doll.

Shirley models her silk pajamas from *Poor Little Rich Girl* (1936).

13" all original. Wearing pleated pique with glued-on white applique. Larger versions of this outfit can be found with three appliques on the bodice. Note the applique design, also found on the coat from *Poor Little Rich Girl*. Rayon dress tag, original pin. Marked on head "SHIRLEY TEMPLE," body marked "USA/13."

13" all original from *Poor Little Rich Girl* (1936). Silk pajamas in blue. Note the variation on the buttons, from the previous photo. Rayon dress tag, original pin. Marked "SHIRLEY TEMPLE" on head and body. *Lorna Erb Collection.*

Blue cotton coat and hat from *Poor Little Rich Girl* (1936). Fits 18" doll. Rayon dress tag. Also available in red. *Lorna Erb Collection.*

Two versions of a pleated cotton dress with rayon tag. This shoulder and collar "loop" detailing can be found on a costume worn in the opening scene of *Poor Little Rich Girl* (1936). Shirley's film costume was designed without the Peter Pan collar.

Red plaid as previously shown. Rayon dress tag. Fits 16" doll.

64

Heavy felt jacket and tam from *Dimples* (1936). Outfit is untagged. Fits 16" doll.

17" all original Texas Ranger. Original pin. Note the vest detailing which varies from size to size.

20" all original Texas Ranger. *Lorna Erb Collection.*

11″ all original Texas Ranger/Cowgirl. Outfit was designed for the 1936 Texas Centennial celebration. Doll is wearing plaid cotton shirt, with real leather vest, chaps and holster, metal gun, imitation brown leather shoes and a felt 10 gallon hat. Hat has a printed band above the brim which reads, "RIDE 'EM COWBOY." Original pin. Marked on head "11/SHIRLEY TEMPLE," body marked "SHIRLEY TEMPLE/11."

Original Texas Ranger/Cowgirl gun.

For the Texas Centennial celebration in 1936, Shirley wears her honorary Texas Ranger outfit. Pictured holding 11″ doll in matching outfit.

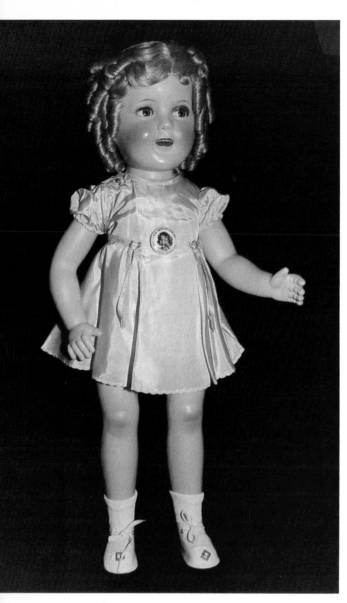

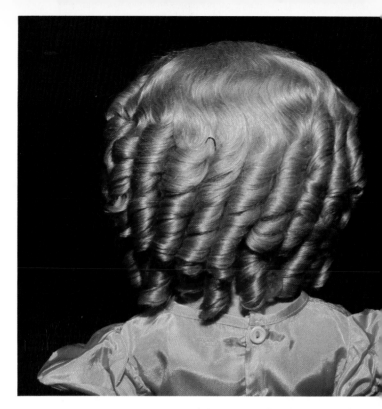

Close-up showing mohair wig detailing, in mint original set.

25" all original from *Stowaway* (1936). Outfit is pink taffeta with silk ribbons. Original movie costume has a ruffled collar. Note the exceptional facial coloring, dark eye shadow and overall expression on this doll. Original pin. *Lorna Erb Collection.*

20" all original from *Stowaway* (1936). Outfit is two-piece linen with brass buttons. Original pin. Marked "SHIRLEY TEMPLE" on head and body. Note that the eyes have crystallized on this doll. See the Care and Restoration chapter for easy repair. *Lorna Erb Collection.*

16" all original in light blue organdy with pink hemstitching and silk ribbons. Rayon "NRA" dress tag, original pin. Marked on head "SHIRLEY TEMPLE/COP. IDEAL/N & T CO.," body marked "SHIRLEY TEMPLE/16."

Doll as previously shown, with original heavy felt coat and hat.

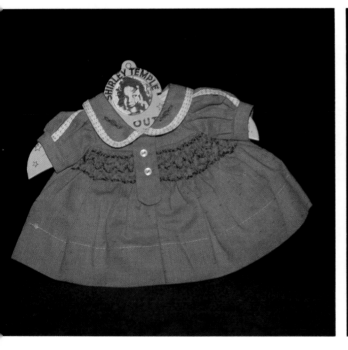

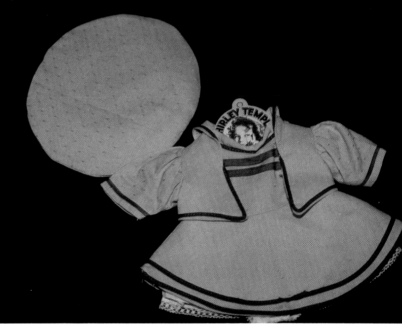

Red pique from *Stowaway* (1936). Rayon dress tag, original cardboard hanger. Fits 16" doll. Also available in blue.

Pique traveling outfit and tam from *Wee Willie Winkie* (1937). Rayon dress tag, original cardboard hanger. Slip/undies can also be seen. Fits 16" doll.

18" from *Wee Willie Winkie* (1937). Wearing long sleeve cotton twill jacket with epaulets, two pockets and six brass buttons. Plaid wool skirt. Tan belt with brass buckle. Rayon tag. Sporan (tassel), fastened in the front of skirt is a replacement. Outfit is missing hat. Marked on head "SHIRLEY TEMPLE/IDEAL N & T CO.," body marked "SHIRLEY TEMPLE/18-." This outfit was only available for the 18" doll.

18" all original from *Wee Willie Winkie*. Shown with 17" and 16" Texas Ranger dolls. *Rita Dubas Collection.*

From *Heidi* (1937), this Dutch girl costume, complete with hand-carved wooden shoes, is perhaps the rarest and most beautifully detailed outfit made for the composition Shirley Temple doll. Pictured is an 18" all original doll in mint condition. Outfit consists of a multi-striped cotton skirt attached to a black velveteen top featuring red braid, lace, and an organdy collar trimmed with a red silk ribbon. Bodice features three rows of embroidered red, yellow and green flowers. Organdy apron has small, red-flocked flowers and multi-colored braided trim and embroidery. Woven cotton dress tag. Organdy slip/undies are tagged "18." Mohair wig, in original set, came parted down the center with braided pigtails, and is tied with red silk ribbons. Tiny soft curls frame the face. Dark eye shadow. Original pin. Doll is marked "SHIRLEY TEMPLE/18" on head and body. Original box from Kresge Department Store, Newark, New Jersey, is dated SEP-1-39 and is priced at $4.98. *Courtesy Muriel Dumais Collection.*

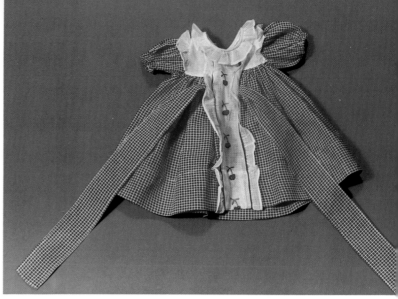

Cotton and organdy dress with embroidery, circa 1935. Streamers tie into a bow at the back. Rayon dress tag. Fits 16" doll.

Cotton school dress, circa 1934. Woven "NRA" tag. Fits 16" doll.

Three original jumpsuits for 16" doll. Rayon dress tags. These outfits were sold separately from the dolls and often were included as a part of the trunk wardrobe.

Opposite:
18" all original from *The Blue Bird* (1939). Wearing felt skirt and vest, organdy blouse and apron. Apron features two glued-on felt blue bird appliques. Rayon dress tag, original pin. Marked on head "SHIRLEY TEMPLE," body marked "U.S.A./SHIRLEY TEMPLE/18." *Marge Meisinger Collection.*

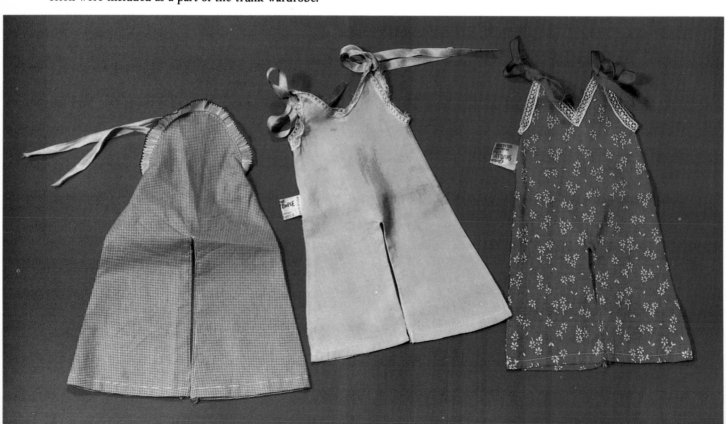

Velveteen coat and hat on original cardboard hanger.
Rayon dress tag. Fits 16" doll.

Apricot dove and floral print, organdy dress with silk ribbon tied at waist. Features delicate lace trim at collar and sleeves. Untagged, on original cardboard hanger. Fits 16" doll.

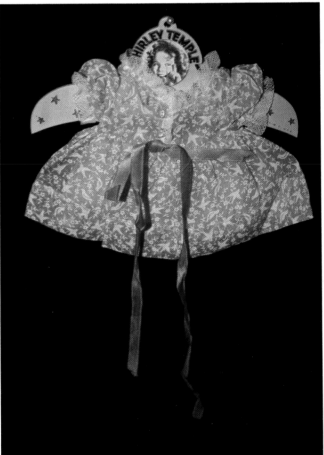

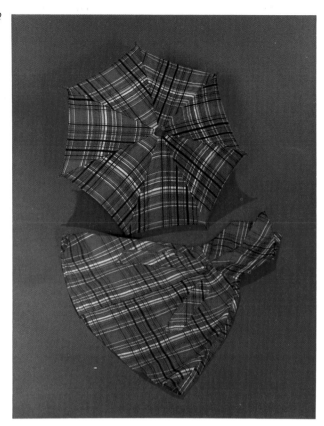

Unusual rain cape with no hood. Rayon "NRA" dress tag. Fits 16" doll.

Cotton sunsuit with matching terry cloth beach cape and hood. Fits 27" doll. Designed by Vogue, expressly for Ideal's composition Shirley Temple doll. Circa 1935.

Plaid rain cape and matching umbrella. Fits 18" doll. Also available in blue.

13" all original. Outfit is blue printed dimity with organdy collar. Rayon "NRA" dress tag, original pin. Marked on head "SHIRLEY TEMPLE," body marked "SHIRLEY TEMPLE/13."

I have such fun curling my
*[Shir]*ley's hair. Now I can always
*[ke]*ep her looking nice.

Shirley Temple

Shirley sets the hair on a 27" doll.

18" all original. Wearing organdy dress with blue flowers printed in fabric. Dress features two heart-shaped, plastic buttons fastened to the bodice. Rayon dress tag, original pin. Marked on head "18/SHIRLEY TEMPLE/IDEAL/COP. N & T CO.," body marked "SHIRLEY TEMPLE."

13″ all original by Reliable, Ideal's Canadian affiliate company. Wearing printed yellow organdy dress with silk ribbon tied at the waist. Dress is tagged "RELIABLE TOY CO. LTD/MADE IN CANADA." Doll is marked on head "SHIRLEY TEMPLE/COP. IDEAL/N & T CO.," body marked "SHIRLEY TEMPLE." Note the exceptional high coloring on cheeks.

Original button which came on the Reliable Shirley Temple doll. Pin reads, "THE WORLD'S DARLING/GENUINE SHIRLEY TEMPLE, A RELIABLE DOLL."

Five original 18″ composition dolls. Doll on left has replaced pin.

Six all original Shirley Temple dolls. From L. to R.: 20"
Little Colonel; 18" *Our Little Girl*; 17" *Texas Ranger*; 16"
Curly Top; 13" *Little Colonel*; and 11" *Curly Top*.

Close-up showing detail of the original cardboard
hanger found on each outfit sold separately.

Trunk and original wardrobe for 13" doll. Shown with
five original tagged outfits, skates and extra shoes.
Hangers are not original.

Vinyl Dolls

1957

12" vinyl, all original with original box and wrist tag. Shown with original plastic "Shirley Temple" script pin. Doll is marked on the back of the head "S.T./12." 1957.

12" vinyl doll in original two piece slip/undies. Tagged "Shirley Temple." Note the hand and feet molding, plus the 1950s synthetic rooted wig.

Side view of the 1957 box.

Side view of another version of the 1957—1958 box.

Close-up showing the original plastic script pin which accompanied all of the 1950s vinyl Shirley Temple dolls.

12″ all original in original box. Doll is wearing pink slip, trimmed with lace and is shown with original wrist tag. 1957.

Three 12″ dolls, all original. L. to R.: *Rebecca Of Sunnybrook Farm*, red heavy felt jumper with rick-rack trim, and another variation from *Rebecca Of Sunnybrook Farm*. Note the red plastic "Shirley Temple" purse and the variation on the shoes.

12" all original. Wearing pink and blue nylon dress with daisy appliques around the bodice and a silk ribbon tied around waist. Shown with original hat, purse and wrist tag. Dress tagged "Shirley Temple." Doll marked "S.T/12." 1958.

15" all original. Wearing red nylon dress with floral detailing at collar and printed in fabric. Doll is shown with original purse and wrist tag. Dress tagged "Shirley Temple." Doll marked "S.T./15." 1958.

15" all original with original box. Doll is shown wearing yellow nylon dress trimmed with lace and ribbons. Note the original script pin and purse. Dress is tagged "Shirley Temple/made by IDEAL TOY CORP." Doll marked "S.T./15." 1958.

Three plastic purses which often came with the 1950s outfits sold separately. Colors include white, red and navy blue.

15" all original in original box. Wearing blue jumper with a red and white gingham blouse. Shown with original plastic script pin and wrist tag. 1960.

17" all original. Wearing yellow nylon party dress. Dress is tagged "Shirley Temple/made by IDEAL TOY CORP." Doll marked "S.T./17." 1957-1958.

Close-up showing wrist tag detailing. "Twinkle Eyes" are the same as "flirty eyes," eyes that move from side to side.

17" all original with original 1960s box. Wearing yellow organdy party dress. Note the variation of the purse. Original pin and wrist tag.

80

19" all original. Outfit is pink nylon and is tagged "Shirley Temple/ made by IDEAL TOY CORP." Note the exceptional rooted wig, twinkle eyes, and another variation of the original purse. 1957.

17" all original as *Heidi.* 1960-1961.

17" all original. Dress is made of pink and blue nylon. Original wig in original set. Brown twinkle eyes. Note the dress tag. Tag reads "Shirley Temple/made by IDEAL TOY CORP." 1958-1959.

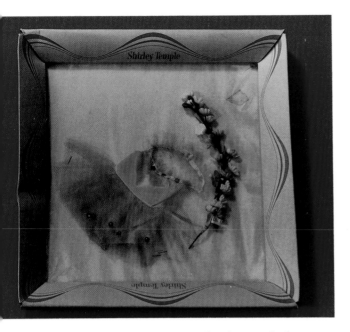

Very early Ballerina outfit available for the 12″ vinyl doll. Made of nylon and tool. 1957-1958.

Nylon dress and jacket with matching purse. Fits 12″ doll. 1959.

Complete outfit-set available in 1958. Set includes straw hat, purse, shoes and socks, undies, jacket, and skirt with attached short sleeve blouse. Fits 12″ doll.

Red corduroy coat and hat. Shown with original purse.
Fits 12" doll. 1958.

This nylon dress from 1958 features an unusual "loop"
detailing on bodice and around the bottom of the
skirt. Fits 12" doll.

Red flannel coat and purse. Fits 12" doll. 1957.

Close-up showing dress tag for the vinyl doll outfits.
Tag is made of rayon.

Gingham with lace detailing from 1958. Fits 12″ doll.

This nylon dress with lace trim was available in several colors and collar variations. 1958.

Cotton and nylon floral jumper and blouse. Fits 12″ doll. 1958.

Cotton with rick-rack trim. Available in blue, green, red and yellow as shown. Fits 12″ doll. 1958.

Variation of the trim detailing from outfit previously shown. 1958.

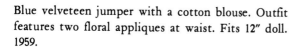
Flannel night coat and cap for a 12″ doll. 1958-1959.

Pink nylon with silk ribbon at waist. Fits 12″ doll. 1958-1959.

Blue velveteen jumper with a cotton blouse. Outfit features two floral appliques at waist. Fits 12″ doll. 1959.

Plaid cotton dress with sash. Fits 12″ doll. 1959-1960.

Rain coat and cape for a 12″ doll. Note how the fashions
for the vinyl doll reflect the styles of the era in which
they were made.

Red felt jumper with a cotton blouse and matching
hat. Jumper features glued-on scotty dog applique,
rick-rack leash and trim. Fits 12″ doll. 1958.

Cotton pajamas and night cap for a 12″ doll. Tagged "IDEAL/Shirley Temple/made by IDEAL TOY CORP." 1959-1960.

Red Cotton sailor dress with matching tam. Fits 12″ doll. 1958.

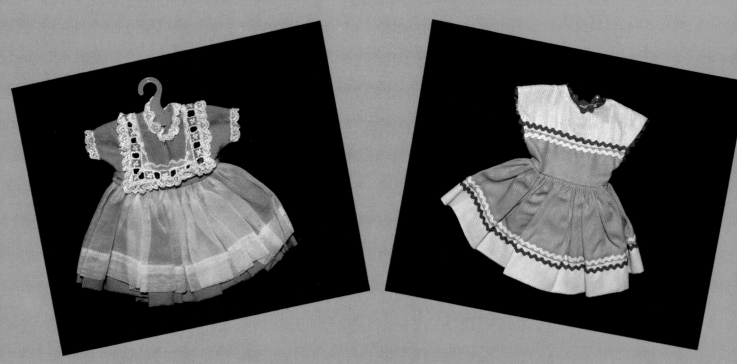

Blue cotton party dress with organdy apron. Outfit features lace lined bodice with interlaced black ribbon detailing. Fits 12″ doll. Outfit was also available in red or green. 1958.

Blue and white, pleated cotton dress with rick-rack trim. Fits 12″ doll. 1958-1959.

Box labels for the outfits sold separately for the 1950s vinyl dolls.

Pink organdy party dress with lace and silk ribbon detailing. Fits 12″ doll. Also available in blue and yellow. 1958.

Original packaged outfit for the 1973 vinyl doll by Ideal. Fits 16″ doll. Costume is from *The Little Colonel*.

1973 packaged outfit from *Captain January*. Fits 16″ doll.

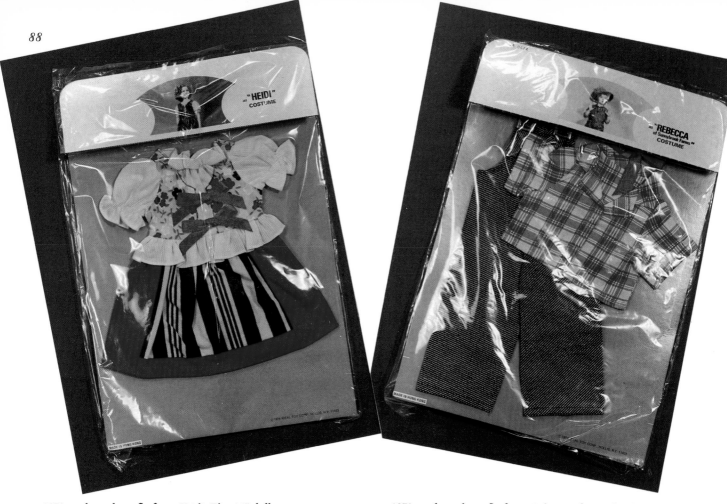

1973 packaged outfit from *Heidi*. Fits 16" doll.

1973 packaged outfit from *Rebecca Of Sunnybrook Farm*. Fits 16" doll.

Boxed *Captain January* outfit for the 1973 vinyl doll by Ideal. Fits 16" doll.

8" *Stowaway* and 12" *The Little Colonel*, by Ideal. 1982.

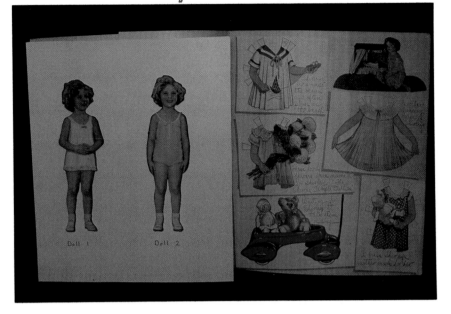

Published by the Saalfield Publishing Co., of Akron, Ohio. This was the very first licensed set of paper dolls made in the image of Shirley Temple. Set is #2112. 1934. Contains four dolls, 8″ in height and thirty outfits to cut-out. Pictured are dolls 1 and 2.

Saalfield #2112. 1934.

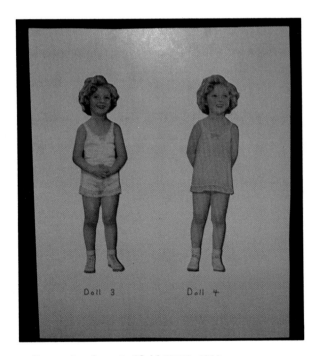

Dolls 3 and 4, from Saalfield #2112. 1934.

Standing doll by Saalfield #1719. 1935.

Saalfield #4435. 1958.

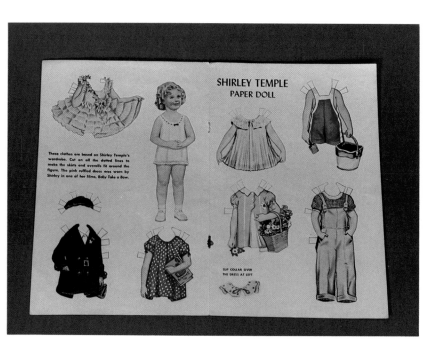

Jack and Jill paper dolls. Reprint of 1934 set. 1959.

Pictured are two 10" dolls from Saalfield #1773. Outfits are from *The Little Colonel* and *Baby Take A Bow*. 1938.

18" standing paper doll. Saalfield #5110. 1959.

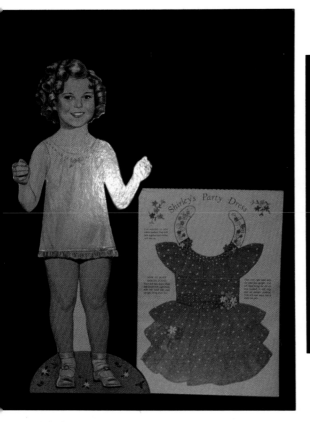

Saalfield #5110. 1959.

18" doll from Saalfield #5110. Shown with uncut party dress. 1959.

Saalfield #1789. 1960.

Saalfield #1789. 1960.

Saalfield #1789. 1960.

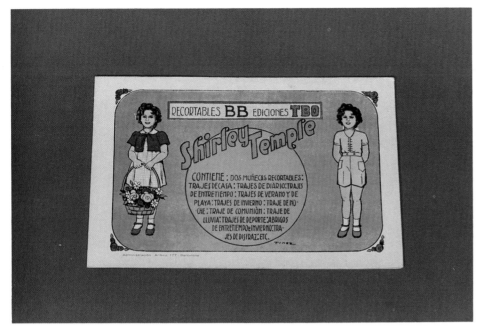

Spanish paper dolls. Circa 1970.

Paper doll book by Whitman Publishing Co. #1986.
Manufactured in 1976.

Whitman paper dolls from 1976. Boxed set shown with
doll and two outfits.

Collectibles

the Story of Shirley Temple by the Saalfield Publishing Co. "Big Little Books" #1089. 1934.

SHIRLEY TEMPLE in THE LITTLE COLONEL. "Big Little Books" by Saalfield #1095. 1935.

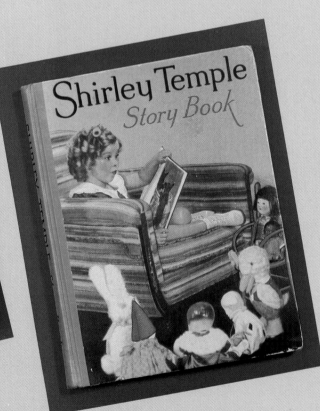

Shirley Temple in The Littlest Rebel. "Big Little Books" by Saalfield #1595. 1935.

Shirley Temple Story Book. Saalfield #1726. 1935.

Shirley Temple at Play. Saalfield #1712. 1935.

Back cover of Saalfield #1712.

Shirley Temple 5 BOOKS ABOUT ME. Saalfield #1730. 1936.

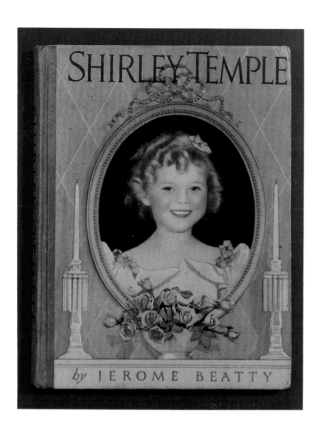

SHIRLEY TEMPLE by Saalfield. 1935.

1935 pressbook from *The Littlest Rebel*. Contains photographs and promotional advertising aimed at theater owners. *Helen Hesson Collection.*

Shirley Temple PASTIME BOX. Saalfield #1732. Contains four activity books. 1937.

SHIRLEY TEMPLE SCRAP BOOK published by Saalfield in 1936. Item #1722.

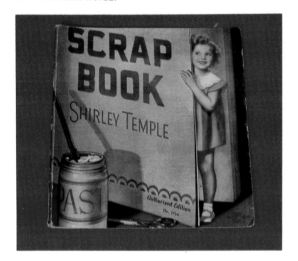

SCRAP BOOK by Saalfield #1714. 1935.

Shirley Temple's Favorite Poems. Published by the Saalfield Publishing Co. #1720. 1936.

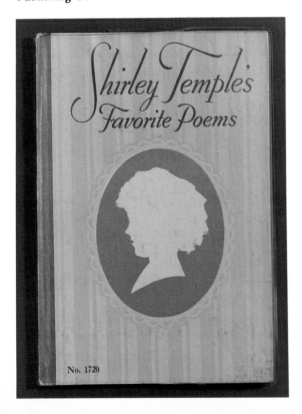

MY LIFE AND TIMES by SHIRLEY TEMPLE. "Big Little Books" by Saalfield #116. 1936.

Shirley Temple Scrap Book by Saalfield #1763. 1937.

Shirley Temple. Printed in Dutch. 1936. *Rita Dubas Collection.*

Interior of the Dutch booklet.

THIS IS MY CRAYON BOOK. Saalfield #1711. 1936.

SHIRLEY TEMPLE A GREAT BIG BOOK TO COLOR. Saalfield #1717. 1936.

Shirley Temple My Book to Color. Saalfield #1768. 1937.

SHIRLEY TEMPLE BLUE BIRD Coloring Book. Published by Saalfield, circa 1939.

Shirley Temple's BUST BOOK. Saalfield #5326. 1958.

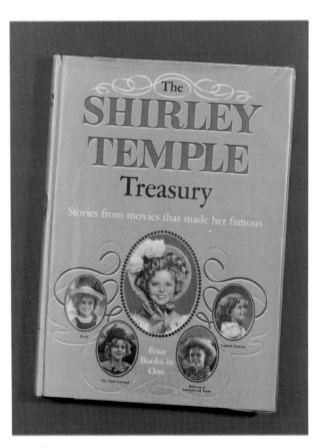

The SHIRLEY TEMPLE Treasury by Random House. 1959.

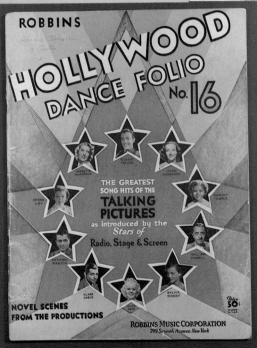

Les Chansons de SHIRLEY (The Songs of SHIRLEY).
French song album. Published by Irving Caesar, Inc.
1936.

SHIRLEY TEMPLE'S Favorite Songs. Published by
Robbins Music Corp. 1937.

Sing with Shirley Temple. Song book album by Sam Fox.
1935.

HOLLYWOOD DANCE FOLIO No.16. Published by
Robbins Music Corp. 1937.

SHIRLEY TEMPLE SONG ALBUM N0.2 Sam Fox
Publishing Co. 1937.

Shirley Temple Song Album. Published by Sam Fox. 1957.

Left: *LITTLE COLONEL* song album by Sam Fox. 1934.
Right: Sheet music "When I'm With You," from *Poor Little Rich Girl.* Sam Fox 1936.

1934 Give-away photograph.

your friend
Shirley Temple

Two-sided cardboard store display. 1934. Measures 15½" tall, 12" wide.

Pen and pencil set manufactured by David Kahn, Inc. of North Bergen, New Jersey. 1930s.

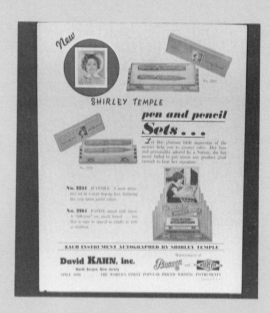

1930 promotional ad for Shirley Temple pen and pencil set.

1930s writing tablet.

Composition book from 1935. Manufactured by the Western Publishing Co.

1930s candy box.

Stationary box manufactured by W.T. & S. Corp. 1936.

Shirley Temple soap in original box. Manufactured by
Kerk Guild Inc. 1930s.

6¾" Austrian figurine. Made of fine china. 1930s. *Rita
Dubas Collection.*

Close-up showing facial molding and curls.

Salt figurines from *Baby Take A Bow*. Unmarked. 1934.

Bisque salt figurine. Manufacturer unknown. Circa 1935.

Sapphire blue "scalloped" glass mug, bowl and pitcher. Given away free with the purchase of one large package of *BISQUICK*. Manufactured by General Mills, Minneapolis, Minn. Items were promoted as a "Sure-Fire Way To Get Your Child To Drink Milk." Glassware was also available with the purchase of *Wheaties* cereal. Items were made by the Hazel Atlas Glass Co. 1935.

Bisque salt figurine in riding habit with dog. Manufacturer unknown. Circa 1935.

Unlicensed 1930s valentine card. *Rita Dubas Collection.*

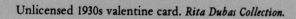

Boxed set of bridge cards manufactured by the U.S. Playing Card Co. 1934. *Rita Dubas Collection.*

Shirley Temple Bridge Cards by the U.S. Playing Card Co. 1934.

Child's hairbow and band. Available in several colors and sizes. Manufactured by the Ribbon Mills Corp. 1934.

Hair Ribbon by the Ribbon Mills Corp. 1934.

Child's dress by Cinderella. This linen sailor dress is tagged "A Cinderella Frock/Shirley Temple/Brand/Made In USA." Dress features swimming fish, printed in fabric. 1930s.

Child's cotton dress by Cinderella. Features animal train appliques. 1960s.

Child's dress made of blue organdy. Dress is tagged "A Nannette Toddler/Shirley Temple/Brand," "#7093/Size 1." Red and white tag shown, reads "THIS EMBLEM IDENTIFIES GENUINE SWISS FABRIC/IMPORTED FROM SWITZERLAND." Blue tag reads "Just like mine/Shirley Temple." Circa 1935.

Close-up of paper tag found on Nannette Toddler child's dress.

Enameled Shirley Temple pin. 1930s. *Rita Dubas Collection.*

Cardboard fan marked "IMPORTE DU JAPON/ PATENT.N0.60596." 1930s.

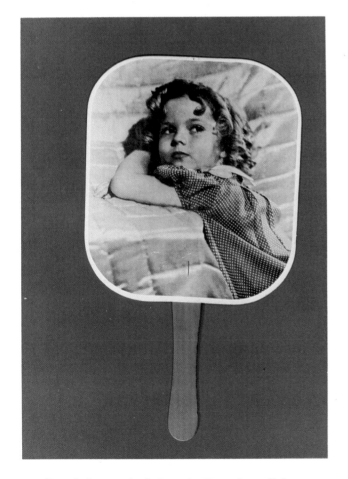

Cardboard fan marked "Movie Fan. Serendipity. N.Y.C." Date unknown.

Super 8 home movie from *War Babies* (1932). Manufactured by Ken Films Inc.

Child's navy blue Shirley Temple hat. 1936. Hat is shown on 36″ vinyl Shirley Temple doll by Ideal, 1959. *Rita Dubas Collection.*

Close-up showing tags for 1936 Shirley Temple hat.

Embroidered pot holders. 5″ square. Circa 1937.

10¼" plate by Nostalgia Collectibles. The first in a series of three is from *Baby Take A Bow*. Edge of plate features embossed ribbons and a band of 24 karat gold. 1983. *Helen Hesson Collection.*

Second plate in a series of three from *Curly Top*. Nostalgia Collectibles. 1983. *Helen Hesson Collection.*

The third plate in the series of three is from *Stand Up And Cheer*. Nostalgia Collectibles. 1983. *Helen Hesson Collection.*

Nostalgia Collectibles introduced another series of plates measuring 8½". Sixth in a series of eight is from *Rebecca of Sunnybrook Farm*. 1983-1984. *Helen Hesson Collection.*

Eighth in a series of eight by Nostalgia. *Wee Willie Winkie.* 1983-1984. *Helen Hesson Collection.*

Shirley Temple dolls from the *Rita Dubas Collection* are shown here, displayed safely behind glass. Dolls remain free from dust build-up and surrounding temperatures remain stable.

Chapter 3

Care and Restoration

With each passing year, it becomes increasingly more difficult to find a "mint," perfect composition doll. Extremely susceptible to cracking and crazing, if left unchecked and improperly cared for, composition can literally deteriorate overnight, effecting not only the appearance of the doll, but also its value. The following preventive measures and precautions will help you to achieve many years of successful enjoyment, hopefully without any major mishaps or damage.

Composition Dolls

Maintaining the condition of a composition doll requires special attention to its surrounding environment. Composition's worst enemies consist of extreme or sudden changes in temperature, dryness, and direct exposure to sunlight.

When storing and displaying, always avoid placing dolls near windows or in direct contact with air conditioners and héating systems. For protection from the elements, whenever possible, dolls should be displayed behind glass. This will also help prevent dust from eventually soiling wigs and clothing. Glass cases should never be air-tight however. During warm summer months, if the air is not allowed to circulate freely, heat can build up inside. Open the display case doors periodically when temperatures start to rise above 80 degrees. A small hole can also be drilled into the bottom of the case to allow air exchange. Ideal temperatures coincide with temperatures in which you yourself feel comfortable. Temperatures of sixty-two to seventy-four degrees are ideal. If your case is equipped with lighting, make sure that the unit is not throwing out to much heat. Use low watt bulbs or a dimmer mechanism. Remember, light bulbs get hot and heat causes damage.

Composition, and all other products made from wood, expand and contract with changes in temperature. Heat causes expansion. Cold temperatures cause contraction. Along with excess dryness, it is this expansion and contraction effect which causes cracking and crazing. During cold winter months, try adding a small glass or jar of regular tap water in an inconspicuous place at the back of the case. This will keep moisture in the air and prevent damage due to dryness. Again, use yourself as a judge. If your own skin is beginning to feel dry and starting to crack from the cold weather, so too is your composition doll. Water level will need to be checked every so often for evaporation.

Storing composition dolls can also be tricky. Surrounding conditions should remain stable. Mid to lower closet shelves prove best, and attics should, for the most part, be avoided altogether. Heat rises!

Dolls should be packed with tissue paper in a sturdy cardboard box. Never use plastic containers or wrap a doll in an air-tight plastic bag. Plastic will not allow wood composition to breath as needed. Also, make sure that doll stands and all other metal items have been completely removed (safety pins, etc.). Moisture and high humidity will cause these items to rust, which eventually will begin to destroy clothing and even the doll itself.

Cleaning a composition doll and minor repairs to crazing of the paint finish and limited cracking, as well as bringing life back into the wig and eyes (which tend to crystallize over the years), is fairly easy to achieve and can be done at home rather simply. You will need the following items;

soft pink eraser	*Johnson's* paste wax
pencil-tip erasers	*Elmer's* wood filler
Nivea lotion	3 in 1 household oil
cotton balls	medium size sewing needle
Q-Tip swabs	rat-tail comb
paper towels	large bath towel

First, and most important, NEVER WASH A COMPOSITION DOLL. Water and most water-based cleaners will severely damage your doll. Some recommend the use of the spray cleaner *Formula 409* if wiped dry immediately after using. I prefer the following technique.

Lightly soiled dolls can easily and safely be cleaned by applying a little *Nivea* lotion to a cotton ball and simply wiping clean. For more heavily soiled dolls, you will be amazed at the years of dirt that can be removed by using an ordinary eraser on the end of a pencil. Rub lightly, using short even strokes. Dirt, crayon marks, scratches, etc., will come off right before your eyes, with no possibility of water seeping down into cracks and ruining your doll. Be careful to change to a new pencil when the eraser begins to wear-down towards the metal band. You don't want to scratch your doll. The smallness of the pencil eraser will enable you to get into tight areas around the eyes, nose, mouth, ears and fingers. You may also use a soft pink eraser, available at any art supply store, for larger areas such as the legs, back, and upper arms. When working on the face, AT ALL COSTS, avoid the painted lower lashes, eyebrows, eye shadow and blush to cheeks. These highlighted areas will rub-off easily. For these areas, and when heavy soil has been removed from the rest of the doll, apply some *Nivea* lotion to a cotton ball and wipe gently. This is safe for cheeks, eyebrows, eye shadow and lips, but again, avoid the lower painted lashes.

When the entire doll has been cleaned with *Nivea* to your satisfaction, wipe dry with a paper towel. Your doll will now have a beautiful shine and look as good as new. To seal and protect, *Johnson's* paste wax can now be added, following normal directions on the packaging. As a safety precaution, rest your doll on a large, folded bath towel while working. It will act as a cushion, should you loose your grip and accidentally drop the doll.

Eyes

Eyes that have become badly crystallized, giving your doll a blank, empty-looking expression, can easily be brought back to life with the use of some 3 in 1 household oil, found at your local hardware center.

First, stand the doll upright so that the eyes are open. You will be working on one eye at a time. Place your index finger firmly on the center of one of the eyes. Grab hold of the doll with your other hand and slowly begin to recline the doll onto your bath towel. Use your index finger firmly, so that the eyes remain open. You may need to try this a few times to get the hang of it. You want your doll resting on her back, with her eyes open. With your free hand, take a good size sewing needle and GENTLY work a tiny hole into the center (iris) of the eye. Use caution and work slowly. You do not want to chip a piece off of this area. After a tiny hole has been made, place a small drop or two, of the 3 in 1 oil, directly over the hole.

Keep the eyes remaining open with your index finger and give the oil a few seconds to seep down into the hole. The eye will now begin to slowly darken, leaving a rather pleasing, almost new result. Apply a little more oil if needed (use sparingly and avoid contact with the composition and clothing). Bring the doll upright again and repeat the procedure with the other eye.

Hair

Mohair wigs can almost always use a little help. Avoid resetting the curls if at all possible. In all areas of restoration, your goal should be to restore, not replace. Some wigs however, will leave you with no other choice. But, if even a hint of the original set exists, this still remains more desirable than resetting or replacing the wig all together.

Use the metal or plastic tip on the end of a rat-tail comb to slightly lift the hair from the head. Most dolls have been boxed away for many years and their wigs have gotten mashed down over time. A little gentle lifting up and away from the head will do wonders. Gently try and bring curls back into a rounded shape with your fingers. Loose split-ends can be sparingly snipped away. If you need to adjust the hair ribbon, be careful as they can easily rip apart if you pull to hard.

Crazing

Crazing and small cracks can be repaired by using *Elmer's* wood filler (available at most hardware stores), on the end of a *Q-Tip* swab. Press filler firmly down into the cracks and wipe excess away with a clean cotton ball. Allow it to dry and repeat as needed, until lines vanish. In most cases, the wood filler will dry to the exact color of the flesh tone paint. If any of the filler has dried before you have a chance to wipe it away, add some *Nivea* lotion to your cotton ball and wipe. Work in small areas at a time. DO NOT attempt to tackle the entire doll at one time. Work slowly and sparingly and you should be successful.

Clothing

Clothing should be washed only by hand and again, only if necessary. Original knife-pleats and fabric stiffness will be washed away along with the dirt so use good judgement. Use a mild detergent and warm water. Rinse well. It is advisable to remove silk ribbons from clothing as they tend to fray quite easily and they can also bleed onto the fabric. After rinsing, gently pat-out the excess water between two towels. Do not ring. Lay the clothing flat and allow to air dry. White tissue paper or a paper towel can be rolled up and tucked into the sleeves to retain original shape. Iron on a cool setting and make sure that clothing is completely dry before replacing it onto the doll.

Doll Hospital

If major work is needed to repair your doll, and you do not consider yourself qualified in the field of restoration, take the time to visit your local doll hospital. You certainly do not want to make a bad thing worse. If no doll hospital can be found in your area, consult the classified section of your favorite doll or collectibles magazine. You will usually find several listings for doll repair.

A few final words. If minor restoration or cleaning is called for, work slowly and take your time. However, if the doll really doesn't need it, don't do it. Don't fix what isn't broken!

Chapter 4

Shirley Temple's Motion Picture Chronology

1

The Runt Page
Educational Film Corporation
Released: 1931
Running time: 10 minutes
Directed by Roy LaVerne
CAST
Lulu Parsnips _____ Shirley Temple
Raymond Bunion _____ Georgie Smith

2

War Babies
Educational Film Corporation
Released: 1932
Running time: 11 minutes
Directed by Charles Lamont
CAST
Charmaine _____ Shirley Temple
Soldier, boyfriend _____ Georgie Smith
Soldier _____ Eugene Butler

3

The Pie Covered Wagon
Educational Film Corporation
Released: 1932
Running time: 10 minutes
Directed by Charles Lamont
CAST
Captive _____ Shirley Temple
Rescuer _____ Georgie Smith
Cowboys and Indians

4

Glad Rags To Riches
Educational Film Corporation
Released: 1932
Running time: 11 minutes
Directed by Charles Lamont
CAST
La Belle Diaperina _____ Shirley Temple
Her Escort _____ Eugene Butler
Maid _____ Marilyn Granas
Director _____ Georgie Smith

5

The Kid's Last Fight
Educational Film Corporation
Released: 1932
Running time: 10 minutes
Directed by Charles Lamont

CAST
Girlfriend _____ Shirley Temple
Diaper Dampsy _____ Georgie Smith
Thug _____ Sidney Kilbrick

6

Kid In Hollywood
Educational Film Corporation
Released: 1932
Running time: 10 minutes
Directed by Charles Lamont
CAST
Morelegs Sweetrick _____ Shirley Temple
Frightwig Von Strumblebum _____ Georgie Smith

7

Pollytix In Washington
Educational Film Corporation
Released: 1932
Running time: 10 minutes
Directed by Charles Lamont
CAST
Political gold-digger _____ Shirley Temple
Cowboy politician _____ Georgie Smith
Other woman _____ Gloria Ann Mack

8

Kid In Africa
Educational Film Corporation
Released: 1932
Running time: 10 minutes
Directed by Charles Lamont
CAST
Madame Cradlebait,
　Mrs. Diaperzan _____ Shirley Temple
Mr. Diaperzan _____ Danny Boone, Jr.

9

Merrily Tours
Educational Film Corporation
Released: 1932
Running time: 22 minutes
Directed by Charles Lamont
CAST
Sonny Rogers _____ Junior Coughlin
Mary Lou Rogers _____ Shirley Temple
Harry Vanderpool _____ Kenneth Howell
Phyllis Dean _____ Mary Blackford
Harry's "stooge" _____ Sidney Miller
Mr. Rogers _____ Harry Myers

Mrs. Rogers _____ Helene Chadwick
Mr. Dean _____ Lloyd Ingraham
Betty _____ Thelma Hill
Mrs. Vanderpool _____ Isabel La Mal

10

Dora's Dunking Doughnuts
Educational Film Corporation
Released: 1933
Running time: 22 minutes
Directed by Harry J. Edwards
CAST
Andy _____ Andy Clyde
Dora _____ Florence Gill
Mrs. Zilch _____ Fern Emmett
Mrs. Blotts _____ Blanche Payson
Mrs. Ipswick _____ Georgia O'Dell
Shirley _____ Shirley Temple
The Meglin Kiddies Band

11

Pardon My Pups
Educational Film Corporation
Released: 1933
Running time: 22 minutes
Directed by Charles Lamont
CAST
Sonny Rogers _____ Junior Coughlin
Mary Lou Rogers _____ Shirley Temple
Henry Vanderpool _____ Kenneth Howell
Mr. Rogers _____ Harry Myers

12

Managed Money
Educational Film Corporation
Released: 1933
Running time: 22 minutes
Directed by Charles Lamont
CAST
Sonny Rogers _____ Frank "Junior" Coughlin
Mary Lou Rogers _____ Shirley Temple
Mr. Rogers _____ Harry Myers
Mrs. Rogers _____ Helene Chadwick

13

What To Do
Educational Film Corporation
Released: 1933
Running time: 22 minutes
Directed by Charles Lamont
CAST
Sonny Rogers _____ Frank Coughlin
Mary Lou Rogers _____ Shirley Temple
Mr. Rogers _____ Harry Myers
Henry Vanderpool _____ Kenneth Howell

14

The Red-Haired Alibi
Tower Productions
Released: 1933
Running time: 71 minutes
Directed by Christy Cabanna
CAST
Lynn Monith _____ Merna Kennedy
Trent Travers _____ Theodore Von Eltz
Rob Shelton _____ Grant Withers
Regan _____ Purnell Pratt
Kente _____ Huntley Gordon
Cocoran _____ Fred Kelsey
Morgan _____ John Vosburgh
Bee Lee _____ Marion Lessing
Gloria _____ Shirley Temple
Margoli _____ Paul Porcasi
Henri _____ Arthur Hoyt

15

Out All Night
Universal Pictures
Released: 1933
Running time: 69 minutes
Directed by Sam Taylor
CAST
Ronald Colgate _____ Slim Summerville
Bonny _____ ZaSu Pitts
Mrs. Colgate _____ Laura Hope Crews
Kate _____ Shirley Grey
Rosemountain _____ Alexandra Carr
David Arnold _____ Rollo Lloyd
Tracy _____ Gene Lewis
Children _____ Shirley Temple
Billy Barty
Phillip Purdy

16

To The Last Man
Paramount
Released: 1933
Running time: 60 minutes
Directed by Henry Hathway
CAST
Lynn Hayden _____ Randolph Scott
Ellen Colby _____ Esther Ralston
Bill Hayden _____ Buster Crabbe
Jed Colby _____ Noah Beery
Jim Daggs _____ Jack LaRue
Neil Standing _____ Barton MacLane
Ann Hayden _____ Gail Patrick
Mark Hayden _____ Egon Brecher
Jeff Morley _____ Fuzzy Knight
Ely Bruce _____ James Engles
Molly Hayden _____ Murial Kirkland
Granny Spelvin _____ Eugenie Besserer

SHIRLEY TEMPLE DOLL

DELIVERED FREE OF CHARGE

Each doll is packed in a special Shirley Temple box, bearing the little star's picture and signature, confirming that it is the one and only Shirley Temple Doll. Each doll wears a celluloid Shirley Temple button which her little owner can proudly wear to school. The doll is 13 inches tall and is officially endorsed by Shirley and her mother.

The doll is the very image of Shirley Temple, with laughing eyes, sparkling teeth, curly, natural hair, winning smile, cute dimple, and dressed exactly as she appears in her latest hit pictures.

An 8 x 10 inch
AUTOGRAPHED PHOTO
OF SHIRLEY TEMPLE SUITABLE FOR FRAMING ENCLOSED WITH EACH DOLL

HERE'S HOW YOU MAY GET THIS GENUINE SHIRLEY TEMPLE DOLL AS YOUR PRIZE

JUST SHOW this magazine to girls you know and see if they don't enjoy it as you do. Go with the girls to their mothers and let them order a subscription through you. When you have secured four new subscriptions (they may choose 8 months for $1.00, or 1 year for $1.50, or 2 years for $2.00), send us the four names and addresses, together with the money you have received for the subscriptions. We will then send you this adorable Shirley Temple Doll, which is all boxed ready for shipment, the instant we receive the FOUR new American Girl subscriptions.

●

ADDRESS:

Department D,

THE AMERICAN GIRL

570 Lexington Avenue

New York, N. Y.

Grandpa Spelvin	Harlan Knight
Pete Garon	John Peter Richmond
Harry Malone	Harry Cording
Judge	Erville Alderson
Sheriff	James Burke
Mary Standing	Shirley Jane Temple

17

Carolina
Fox Film Corp.
Released: 1933
Running time: 63 minutes
Directed by Henry King
CAST

Joanna	Janet Gaynor
Bob Connelly	Lionel Barrymore
Will Connelly	Robert Young
Mrs. Connelly	Henrietta Crosman
Allen	Richard Cromwell
Virginia	Mona Barrie
Scipio	Stepin Fetchit
Richards	Russell Simpson
Harry	Ronnie Cosbey
Jackie	Jackie Cosbey
Geraldine	Almeda Fowler

(Shirley Temple received no screen credit)

18

Mandalay
Warner Brothers First National
Released: 1933
Running time: 60 minutes
Directed by Michael Curtiz
CAST

Tanya	Kay Francis
Tony Evans	Ricardo Cortez
Nick	Warner Oland Dr.
Gregory Burton	Lyle Talbot
Mrs. Peters	Ruth Donnelly
Commissioner	Reginald Owen
Captain	David Torrence
The Countess	Rafaela Ottiano
Col. Dawson Ames	Holliwell Hobbes
Mr. Abernathie	Etienne Girardot
Mr. Peters	Lucien Littlefield
Mrs. Kleinschmidt	Bodil Rosing
Mr. Kleinschmidt	Herman Bing
Henry P. Warren	Harry C. Bradley
Ram Singh	James B. Leong
Betty Shaw	Shirley Temple
Louisa Mae Harrington	Lillian Harmer
Van Brinker	Torben Meyer

19

As The Earth Turns
Warner Brothers
Released: 1933

Running time : 60 minutes
Directed by Alfred E. Green
CAST

Mrs. Janowski	Sarah Padden
Stan Janowski	Donald Woods
Janowski	Egon Brecher
Manuel	David Durand
Maria	Cora Sue Collins
Louise	Gloria Fisher
Mark Shaw	David Landau
Cora Shaw	Clara Blandick
Jen Shaw	Jean Muir
Doris	Dorothy Appleby
Ed Shaw	Russell Hardie
Ollie Shaw	William Janney
Bunny Shaw	Dorothy Gray
John Shaw	Wally Albright
George Shaw	Arthur Hohl
Mil Shaw	Dorothy Peterson
Margaret	Emily Lowry
Esther Shaw	Marilyn Knowlden
Junior Shaw	George Billings
Betty Shaw	Shirley Temple
Sister	Joyce Kay

20

New Deal Rhythm
Paramount
Released: 1933
CAST
Charles "Buddy" Rogers
Marjorie Main
Shirley Temple

21

Stand Up And Cheer
Fox Film Corp.
Released: 1934
Running time: 69 minutes
Directed by Hamilton McFadden
CAST

Lawrence Cromwell	Warner Baxter
Mary Adams	Madge Evans
Jimmy Dugan	James Dunn
as herself	Sylvia Froos
as himself	John Boles
John Harley	Arthur Byron
Secretary to the President	Ralph Morgan
Shirley Dugan	Shirley Temple
as herself	Aunt Jemima (Tess Gardell)
Senators Danforth and Short	Mitchell & Durant
as himself	Dick Foran
Dinwiddie	Nigel Bruce
Hillbilly	"Skins" Miller
as himself	Stepin Fetchit

Now I'll Tell
Fox Film Corp.
Released: 1934
Running time: 75 minutes
Directed by Edwin Burke
CAST

Murry Golden	Spencer Tracy
Virginia	Helen Twelvetrees
Peggy	Alice Faye
Mositer	Robert Gleckler
Doran	Henry O'Neill
Freddie	Hobart Cavanaugh
Hart	G.P. Huntley, Jr.
Doran's daughter	Shirley Temple
Doran's son	Ronald Cosby
Traylor	Ray Cooke
Curtis	Frank Marlowe
Davis	Clarence Wilson
Wynne	Barbara Weeks
Joe	Theodore Newton
Peppo	Vince Barnett
Honey Smith	Jim Donlan

23

Change Of Heart
Fox Film Corp.
Released: 1934
Running time: 76 minutes
Directed by John G. Blystone
CAST

Shirley	Shirley Temple
Catherine Furness	Janet Gaynor
Chris Thring	Charles Farrell
Mack McGowan	James Dunn
Madge Rountree	Ginger Rogers
Harriett Hawkins	Beryl Mercer
Mr. Kreutzmann	Gustav Von Seyffertitz
Greta Hailstrom	Irene Franklin
T.P. McGowan	Fiske O'Hara
Mrs. Mockby, Jr.	Drue Leyton
Mrs. Rountree	Mary Carr
Howard Jackson	Kenneth Thomson
Mrs. Mockby	Nella Walker
Phyllis Carmichael	Barbara Barondess

24

Little Miss Marker
Paramount
Released: 1934
Running time: 70 minutes
Directed by Alexander Hall
CAST

Miss Marker (Martha, Marky)	Shirley Temple
Sorrowful Jones	Adolphe Menjou
Bangles Carson	Dorothy Dell
Big Steve	Charles Bickford
Regret	Lynne Overman
Doc Chesley	Frank McGlynn, Sr.
Sun Rise	Jack Sheehan
Grinder	Gary Owen
Sleep'n'Eat, Dizzy Memphis	Willie Best
Eddie	Puggy White
Benny the Gouge	Sam Hardy
Buggs	Tammany Young
Marky's father	Edward Earle
Sore Toe	John Kelly
Canvas Back	Warren Hymer
Dr. Ingalls	Frank Conroy
Reardon	James Burke
Sarah	Mildred Gover
Mrs. Walsh	Lucille Ward
Doctor	Craufurd Kent
Head of Home Finding Society	Nora Cecil

25

Baby Take A Bow
Fox Film Corp.
Released: 1934
Running time: 76 minutes
Directed by Harry Lachman
CAST

Eddie Ellison	James Dunn
Kay Ellison	Claire Trevor
Shirley	Shirley Temple
Welch	Alan Dinehart
Larry Scott	Ray Walker
Jane	Dorothy Libaire
Trigger Stone	Ralph Harolde
Flannigan	James Flavin
Mr. Carson	Richard Tucker
Mrs. Carson	Olive Tell
Rag Picker	John Alexander

26

Now And Forever
Paramount
Released: 1934
Running time: 70 minutes
Directed by Harry Hathaway
CAST

Jerry Day	Gary Cooper
Toni Carstairs	Carole Lombard
Pennie (Penelope Day)	Shirley Temple
Felix Evans	Sir Guy Standing
Mrs. J.H.P. Crane	Charlotte Granville
James Higginson	Gilbert Emery
Mr. Clark	Henry Kolker
Inspector	Andre' Cheron
Mr. Ling	Tetsu Komai
Daschund	Dog Buster

27

Bright Eyes
Fox Film Corp.
Released: 1934
Running time: 84 minutes
Directed by David Butler
CAST
Shirley Blake ——————————— Shirley Temple
Loop Merritt ——————————— James Dunn
Mrs. Higgins ——————————— James Darwell
Adele Martin ——————————— Judith Allen
Mary Blake ——————————— Lois Wilson
Uncle Ned Smith——————————— Charles Sellon
Thomas ——————————— Walter Johnson
Joy Smyth ——————————— Jane Withers
J. Wellington Smyth ——————— Theodore von Eltz
Anita Smyth——————————— Dorothy Christy
Higgins ——————————— Brandon Hurst
Judge Thompson ——————————— George Irving
Airplane friend (Tex) ——————————David O'Brien

28

The Little Colonel
Fox Film Corp.
Released: 1934
Running time: 80 minutes
Directed by David Butler
CAST
Lloyd Sherman
   (The Little Colonel) ——————— Shirley Temple
Col. Lloyd ——————————— Lionel Barrymore
Elizabeth Lloyd Shermen ——————Evelyn Venable
Jack Sherman——————————— John Lodge
Swazey ——————————— Sidney Blackmer
Hull ——————————— Alden Chase
Dr. Scott ——————————— William Burress
Mom Beck ——————————— Hattie McDaniel
Maria ——————————— Geneva Williams
May Lily ——————————— Avonne Jackson
Henry Clay ——————————— Nyanza Potts, Jr.
Nebler ——————————— Frank Darien
Walker ——————————— Bill Robinson

29

Our Little Girl
Fox Film Corp.
Released: 1935
Running time: 63 minutes
Directed by John Robertson
CAST
Molly Middleton ——————————— Shirley Temple
Elsa Middleton ———————————Rosemary Ames
Dr. Donald Middleton——————————Joel McCrea
Rolfe Brent ——————————— Lyle Talbot
Sarah Boynton ——————————— Erin O'Brien-Moore
Circus performer (clown) ——————— Poodles Hanneford
Amy ———————————Margaret Armstrong

Alice ——————————— Rita Owin
Jackson——————————Leonard Carey
Mr. Tramp——————————J. Farrell MacDonald
Leyton ——————————— Jack Baxley

30

Curly Top
Fox Film Corp.
Released: 1935
Running time: 75 minutes
Directed by Irving Cummings
CAST
Elizabeth Blair (Betsy)——————————Shirley Temple
Edward Morgan——————————John Boles
Mary Blair ———————————Rochelle Hudson
Mrs. Denham——————————— Jane Darwell
Mrs. Higgins ———————————Rafaela Ottiano
Aunt Genevieve——————————— Esther Dale
Morgan's butler——————————Arthur Treacher
Mr. Wyckoff ——————————— Etienne Giardot
Jimmie Rogers ———————————Maurice Murphy

31

The Littlest Rebel
Twentieth Century-Fox
Released: 1935
Running time: 73 minutes
Directed by David Butler
CAST
Virginia Houston Cary ——————— Shirley Temple
Captain Herbert Cary——————————John Boles
Colonel Morrison——————————Jack Holt
Mrs. Cary ——————————— Karen Morley
Uncle Billy ———————————Bill Robinson
Sergeant Dudley ———————————Guinn Williams
James Henry ———————————Willie Best
President Lincoln——————————— Frank McGlynn, Sr.
Mammy ———————————Bessie Lyle
Sally Ann ———————————Hannah Washington

32

Captain January
Twentieth Century-Fox
Released: 1936
Running time: 76 minutes
Directed by David Butler
CAST
Star———————————Shirley Temple
Captain January ———————————Guy Kibbee
Mary Marshall ——————————— June Lang
Captain Nazro ——————————— Slim Summerville
Paul Rogers ———————————Buddy Ebsen
Agatha Morgan ——————————— Sara Haden
Eliza Croft ——————————— Jane Darwell
Cyril Morgan——————————Jerry Tucker
Mrs. John Mason ———————————Nella Walker
John Mason ——————————— George Irving

WARNING!

NOTICE TO DEALERS

SHIRLEY TEMPLE
AND HER DOLL

●

On September 21st, 1935, a decision was rendered in the Supreme Court of the State of New York, against a doll company, in a suit brought by Shirley Temple and by Ideal Novelty & Toy Company. Shirley Temple complained that said doll company was putting out a doll, without her license and permission, which deceptively resembled the well known and genuine "Shirley Temple" doll which Ideal Novelty & Toy Company is exclusively licensed to manufacture and sell. Ideal Novelty & Toy Company complained of unfair competition, because the dolls put out by said doll company were close imitations of the genuine "Shirley Temple" doll.

The decision of the Supreme Court granted a temporary injunction against said doll company and in favor of Shirley Temple and Ideal Novelty & Toy Company. The rights of Shirley Temple were based upon Sections 50 and 51 of the Civil Rights Law of the State of New York. The rights of Ideal Novelty & Toy Company were based upon the general principles of unfair competition.

The suit against said doll company was brought as a test case, and in order to restrain the sale of various unfair imitations of the genuine "Shirley Temple" dolls which have recently appeared on the market. It is not the desire of Ideal Novelty & Toy Company to bring suit against members of the trade or to disturb its relations with its customers. Nevertheless, Shirley Temple, through her duly appointed guardian, is a highly interested party in this matter, because Ideal Novelty & Toy Company pays a royalty to Shirley Temple upon every genuine "Shirley Temple" doll.

We are addressing this letter to the trade because our attention has been called to numerous imitations of the genuine "Shirley Temple" dolls which have recently appeared upon the market. It is the opinion of our counsel that every dealer who handles an infringing doll is liable both to Shirley Temple and to Ideal Novelty & Toy Company, for an injunction, and also for an award of profits and damages. Suit in order to collect profits and damages can be instituted either by Shirley Temple, or by Ideal Novelty & Toy Company, or by both of them.

We are bringing this matter to your attention, in order to request your cooperation so that you will not handle imitations of the genuine "Shirley Temple" doll.

MOCK & BLUM

ATTORNEYS FOR PLAINTIFF

IDEAL NOVELTY & TOY CO

LONG ISLAND CITY, N. Y.

New York City Office: 200 FIFTH AVENUE

Deputy Sheriff	James Farley
Old sailor	Si Jenks
East Indian	John Carradine
Nurse	Mary McLaren
Messenger boy	Billy Benedict

33

Poor Little Rich Girl
Twentieth Century-Fox
Released: 1936
Running time: 72 minutes
Directed by Irving Cummings
CAST

Barbara Barry	Shirley Temple
Jerry Dolan	Alice Faye
Margaret Allen	Gloria Stuart
Jimmy Dolan	Jack Haley
Richard Barry	Michael Whalen
Collins	Sara Haden
Woodward	Jane Darwell
Simon Peck	Claude Gillingwater
Tony	Henry Armetta
Percival Gooch	Arthur Hoyt
Flagin	John Wray
George Hathaway	Paul Stanton
Stebbins	Charles Coleman
Ferguson	John Kelly
Dan Ward	Tyler Brooke
Tony's wife	Mathilde Comont
Freckles	Leonard Kilbrick
Soloist	Dick Webster
Announcer	Bill Ray
Announcer	Gayne Whitman

34

Dimples
Twentieth Century-Fox
Released: 1936
Running time: 78 minutes
Directed by William A. Seiter
CAST

Sylvia Dolores Appleby(Dimples)	Shirley Temple
Professor Appleby	Frank Morgan
Mrs. Caroline Drew	Helen Westley
Allen Drew	Robert Kent
Betty Loring	Delma Byron
Cleo Marsh	Astrid Allwyn
Cicero	Stepin Fetchit
Colonel Loring	Berton Churchill
Mr. St. Clair	Paul Stanton
Hawkins	Julius Tannen
Richards	John Carradine
Proprietor	Herman Bing
Rufus	Billy McClain
Uncle Tom	Jack Clifford
Topsy	Betty Jean Hainey
Pawnbroker	Arthur Aylesworth
Proprietor's wife	Greta Meyer

Stowaway
Twentieth Century-Fox
Released: 1936
Running time: 87 minutes
Directed by William A. Seiter
CAST

Ching-Ching	Shirley Temple
Tommy Randall	Robert Young
Susan Parker	Alice Faye
The Colonel	Eugene Pallette
Mrs. Hope	Helen Westley
Atkins	Arthur Treacher
Judge Booth	J. Edward Bromberg
Kay Swift	Astrid Allwyn
Richard Hope	Allen Lane
Captain	Robert Greig
Dora Day	Jane Regan
First Mate	Julius Tannen
Chang	Willie Fung
Sun Lo	Phillip Ahn
Second Mate	Paul McVey
Mrs. Kruikshank	Helen Jerome Eddy
Alfred Kruikshank	William Stack
Latchee Lee	Honorable Wu

36

Wee Willie Winkie
Twentieth Century-Fox
Released: 1937
Running time: 105 minutes
Directed by John Ford
CAST

Pricilla Williams	Shirley Temple
Sergeant MacDuff	Victor McLaglen
Colonel Williams	C. Aubrey Smith
Joyce Williams	June Lang
Lt. Brandes "Coppy"	Michael Whalen
Khoda Khan	Cesar Romero
Mrs. Allardyce	Constance Collier
Private Mott	Douglas Scott
Captain Bibberbeigh	Gavin Muir
Mohammet Dihn	Willie Fung
Bagby	Brandon Hurst
Major Allardyce	Lionel pape
Pipe Major Sneath	Clyde Cook
Elsie Allardyce	Lauri Beatty
Major General Hammond	Lionel Braham

37

Heidi
Twentieth Century-Fox
Released: 1937
Running time: 87 minutes
Directed by Allan Dwan
CAST

Heidi	Shirley Temple

126

Adolph Kramer	Jean Hersholt
Andrews	Arthur Treacher
Blind Anna	Helen Westley
Elsa	Pauline Moore
Pastor Schultz	Thomas Beck
Fraulein Rottenmeier	Mary Nash
Herr Sesemann	Sidney Blackmer
Aunt Dete	Mady Christians
Police Captain	Sig Rumann
Clara Sesemann	Marcia Mae Jones

38

Rebecca Of Sunnybrook Farm
Twentieth Century-Fox
Released: 1938
Running time: 80 minutes
Directed by Allan Dwan
CAST

Rebecca Winstead	Shirley Temple
Anthony Kent	Randolph Scott
Orville Smithers	Jack Haley
Gwenn Warren	Gloria Stuart
Lola Lee	Phyllis Brooks
Aunt Miranda Wilkins	Helen Westley
Homer Busby	Slim Summerville
Aloysius	Bill Robinson
as themselves	Raymond Scott
Quintet Purvis	Alan Dinehart
Dr. Hill	J.Edward Bromberg
Receptionist	Dixie Dunbar
Mug	Paul Hurst
Henry Kipper	William Demarest
Melba	Ruth Gillette
Cyrus Bartlett	Paul Harvey

39

Little Miss Broadway
Twentieth Century-Fox
Released: 1938
Running time: 70 minutes
Directed by Irving Cummings
CAST

Betsy Brown	Shirley Temple
Roger Wendling	George Murphy
Jimmy Clayton	Jimmy Durante
Barbara Shea	Phyllis Brooks
Sarah Wendling	Edna Mae Oliver
Fiske	George Barbier
Pop Shea	Edward Ellis
Miss Hutchins	Jane Darwell
Ole	El Brendel
Willoughby Wendling	Donald Meek
Flossie	Patricia Wilder
Judge	Claude Gillingwater, Sr.
as themselves	George & Olive Brasno
Mike Brody	Charles Williams
Simmons	Charles Coleman

Perry	Russell Hicks
as themselves	Brian Sisters
Guests	Brewster Twins
Detective	Claire DuBrey
Miles	Robert Gleckler
Pool	C.Montague Shaw
Scully	Frank Dae
Taxi driver	Ben Weldon

40

Just Around The Corner
Twentieth Century-Fox
Released: 1938
Running time: 70 minutes
Directed by Irving Cummings
CAST

Penny Hale	Shirley Temple
Jeff Hale	Charles Farrell
Kitty	Joan Davis
Lola	Amanda Duff
Corporal Jones	Bill Robinson
Gus	Bert Lahr
Waters	Franklin Pangborn
Aunt Julia Ramsby	Cora Witherspoon
Samuel G. Henshaw	Claude Gillingwater, Sr.
Milton Ramsby	Bennie Bartlett
Reporter	Hal K. Dawson

41

The Little Princess
Twentieth Century-Fox
Released: 1939
Running time: 93 minutes
Directed by Walter Lang
CAST

Sara Crewe	Shirley Temple
Geoffrey Hamilton	Richard Greene
Miss Rose	Anita Louise
Captain Crewe	Ian Hunter
Ran Dass	Cesar Romero
Bertie	Arthur Treacher
Miss Minchin	Mary Nash
Becky	Sybil Jason
Lord Wickham	Miles Mander
Lavinia	Marcia Mae Jones
Queen Victoria	Beryl Mercer
Jessie	Deidre Gale
Ermengarde	Ira Stevens

42

Susannah Of The Mounties
Twentieth Century-Fox
Released: 1939
Running time: 79 minutes
Directed by William A. Seiter
CAST

Susannah Sheldon	Shirley Temple
Monty	Randolph Scott
Vicky Standing	Margaret Lockwood
Little Chief	Martin Goodrider
Pat O'Hannegan	J. Farrell MacDonald
Chief Big Eagle	Maurice Moscovich
Supt. Andrew Standing	Moroni Olsen
Wolf Pelt	Victor Jory
Harlan Chambers	Lester Matthews
Randall	Leyland Hodgson
Doctor	Herbert Evans
Williams	Jack Luden
Sergeant McGregor	Charles Irwin
Corporal Piggot	John Sutton
Chief	Chief Big Tree

43

The Blue Bird

Twentieth CenturyFox
Released: 1940
Running time: 83 minutes
Directed by Walter Lang
CAST

Mytyl	Shirley Temple
Mummy Tyl	Spring Byington
Mr. Luxury	Nigel Bruce
Tylette the cat	Gale Sondergaard
Tylo the dog	Eddie Collins
Angela Berlingot	Sybil Jason
Fairy Berylune	Jessie Ralph
Light	Helen Ericson
Tyltyl	Johnny Russell
Mrs. Luxury	Laura Hope Crews
Daddy Tyl	Russell Hicks
Granny Tyl	Cecilia Loftus
Grandpa Tyl	Al Shean
Studious boy	Gene Reynolds
Mrs. Berligot	Leona Roberts
Wilheim	Stansey Andrews
Cypress	Dorothy Dearing
Caller of Roll	Frank Dawson
Nurse	Claire DuBrey
Wild Plum Tree	Sterling Holloway
Father Time	Thurston Hall
Oak Tree	Edwin Maxwell

44

Young People

Twentieth Century Fox
Released: 1940
Running time: 85 minutes
Directed by Allan Dwan
CAST

Wendy	Shirley Temple
Joe Ballantine	Jack Oakie
Kitty Ballantine	Charlotte Greenwood
Marilyn	Arleen Whelan

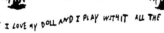

LOOK What Shirley Temple has for YOU

Thousands of girls have seen Shirley Temple's curly head bob in a fast dance . . and watched her pretty face beam with a radiant smile . . or seen her big hazel eyes twinkle with laughter.

Now every girl can have a doll that looks exactly like Shirley. Her natural hair. Laughing eyes. Winning smile. Cute dimples. Even the pleated dress is just like one Shirley wears in a recent hit picture.

This 13-inch doll is sent to you in a handsome Shirley Temple box. What fun you'll have opening it to find an 8-by-11-inch autographed picture of Shirley! How proud you'll be to wear the celluloid Shirley Temple button given with every doll!

THIS DOLL FREE WITH CHILD LIFE

You'll not only get this beautiful doll, but with a year's subscription to CHILD LIFE you will also receive scores of the best stories of mystery, adventure, fun and history available by todays foremost juvenile authors. You'll be as delighted with these fascinating tales as you will be with the exciting games, puzzles, contests, cutouts, hobbies, nature studies, movietown news, travel tales, sewing and cooking lessons that are packed in each colorful issue of CHILD LIFE.

Don't miss this outstanding offer!

HOW TO GET THIS SHIRLEY TEMPLE DOLL

To have a Shirley Temple doll of your very own, just send in two 1-year subscriptions to Child Life at the new low price of $2.50 each. The doll, completely packed as listed here, will be sent to you FREE. There are three other ways to secure this doll. You may send in four 6-month subscriptions at $1.25 each ($5 in all); or one 3-year at $5 and one 6-month at $1.25 ($6.25 in all) or one 3-year at $5 and one 1-year at $2.50 ($7.50 in all). New or renewal subscriptions count. Only one 3-year order at $5 or any subscriptions sent in before October 20, 1936 will not entitle you to the doll. Hurry. Send in your orders at once!

Mike Shea	George Montgomery
Hester Appleby	Kathleen Howard
Dakin	Minor Watson
Fred Willard	Frank Swann
Jeb	Frank Sully
Mrs. Stinchfield	Sara Edwards
Marie Liggett	Mae Marsh
Otis	Irving Bacon
Doorman	Arthur Aylesworth
Station Master	Olin Howland
Stage Manager	Billy Wayne
Dave	Harry Tyler
Tommy	Darryl Hickman
Mary Ann	Shirley Mills
Susie	Diane Fisher
Jerry Dakin	Bobby Anderson
Eddie	Ted North

45

Kathleen
Metro-Goldwyn-Mayer
Released: 1941
Running time: 85 minutes
Directed by Harold S. Bucquet
CAST

Kathleen Davis	Shirley Temple
John Davis	Herbert Marshall
Dr. A. Martha Kent	Laraine Day
Lorraine Bennett	Gail Patrick
Mr. Schoner	Felix Bressart
Mrs. Farrell	Nella Walker
Dr. Montague Foster	Lloyd Corrigan
Jarvis	Guy Bellis
Miss Bewley	Fern Emmett
Policeman	Wade Boteler
Manager	Charles Judels
Maid	Else Argal
Margaret	Margaret Bert
Sign poster	Joe Yule
Moving men	James Flavin, Monty Collins

46

Miss Annie Rooney
United Artists
Released: 1942
Running time: 85 minutes
Directed by Edwin L. Marin
CAST

Annie Rooney	Shirley Temple
Tim Rooney	William Gargan
Grandpop	Guy Kibbee
Marty	Dickie Moore
Myrtle	Peggy Ryan
Joey	Ronald DuPree
Mrs. White	Gloria Holden
Mr. White	Jonathan Hale
Mrs. Metz	Mary Field

Burns	George Lloyd
Madam Sylvia	Jan Buckingham
Mrs. Thomas	Selmer Jackson
Stella Bainbridge	June Lockhart
Sidney	Charles Coleman
Policeman	Edgar Dearing
Myrtle's mother	Virginia Sale
Audrey Hollis	Shirley Mills

47

Since You Went Away
United Artists
Released: 1944
Running time: 172 minutes
Directed by John Cromwell
CAST

Anne Hilton	Claudette Colbert
Lt. Anthony Willett	Joseph Cotten
Col. Smollet	Monty Woolley
Jane	Jennifer Jones
Bridget	Shirley Temple
Fidelia	Hattie McDaniel
Gladys Brown	Jane Devlin
Mr. Mahoney	Lloyd Corrigan
Emily Hawkins	Agnes Moorehead
Corp. William G. Smollett, II	Robert Walker
Johnny Mahoney	Jackie Moran
Harold Smith	Guy Madison
Clergyman	Lionel Barrymore
Danny Williams	Craig Stevens
Dr. Sigmund Golden	Albert Basserman
Lt. Solomon	Keenan Wynn
Zofia Kislowska	Nazimova

48

I'll Be Seeing You
United Artists
Released: 1944
Running time: 82 minutes
Directed by William Dieterle
CAST

Mary Marshall	Ginger Rogers
Zachary Morgan	Joseph Cotten
Barbara Marshall	Shirley Temple
Mrs. Marshall	Spring Byington
Mr. Marshall	Tom Tully
Swanson	Chill Wills
Lt. Bruce	Dare Harris
Sailor on the train	Kenny Bowers
Hawker	Olin Howland
Salesgirl	Dorothy Stone
Paratrooper	John James
Charlie Hartman	Eddie Hall
Sailor in coffee shop	Joe Haworth
Counterman	Jack Carr
Soldier father on train	Bob Meredith

49

Kiss And Tell
Columbia
Released: 1945
Running time: 90 minutes
Directed by Richard Wallace
CAST

Corliss Archer	Shirley Temple
Dexter Franklin	Jerome Courtland
Mr. Archer	Walter Abel
Mrs. Archer	Katharine Alexander
Uncle George	Robert Benchley
Mr. Franklin	Porter Hall
Mrs. Franklin	Edna Holland
Mildred Pringle	Virginia Welles
Mr. Pringle	Tom Tully
Mrs. Pringle	Mary Phillips
Raymond Pringle	Darryl Hickman
Private Jimmy Earhart	Scott McKay
Lenny Archer	Scott Elliott
Louise	Kathryn Card

50

Honeymoon
RKO
Released: 1947
Running time: 74 minutes
Directed by William Keighley
CAST

Barbara Olmstead	Shirley Temple
David Flanner	Franchot Tone
Phil Vaughn	Guy Madison
Raquel Mendoza	Lina Romay
Prescott	Gene Lockhart
Senora Mendoza	Corinna Mura
Crenshaw	Grant Mitchell
Registrar	Manual Arvide
Dr. Diego	Jose R. Goula

51

The Bachelor and the Bobby-Soxer
RKO
Released: 1947
Running time: 93 minutes
Directed by Irving Reis
CAST

Dick	Cary Grant
Margaret	Myrna Loy
Susan	Shirley Temple
Tommy	Rudy Vallee
Beemish	Ray Collins
Thaddeus	Harry Davenport
Jerry	Johnny Sands
Tony	Don Beddoe
Bessie	Lillian Randolph
Agnes Prescott	Veda Ann Borg
Walters	Dan Tobin

Judge Treadwell	Ransom Sherman
Winters	William Bakewell
Melvin	Irving Bacon
Perry	Ian Bernard
Florence	Carol Hughes
Anthony Herman	William Hall

52

That Hagen Girl
Warner Brothers First National
Released: 1947
Running time: 83 minutes
Directed by Peter Godfrey
CAST

Mary Hagen	Shirley Temple
Tom Bates	Ronald Reagan
Minta Hagen	Dorothy Peterson
Jim Hagen	Charles Kemper
Ken Freneau	Rory Calhoun
Sharon Bailey	Jean Porter
Molly Freneau	Nella Walker
Selma Delaney	Winifred Harris
Cora	Ruth Robinson
Julia Kane	Lois Maxwell
Dewey Koons	Conrad Janis
Christine Delaney	Penny Edwards
Judge Merrivale	Harry Davenport

53

Fort Apache
Argosy Pictures, RKO
Released: 1948
Running time: 127 minutes
Directed by John Ford
CAST

Captain York	John Wayne
Lt.Col.Owen Thursday	Henry Fonda
Philadelphia Thursday	Shirley Temple
Sergeant Beaufort	Pedro Armendariz
Sergeant O'Rourke	Ward Bond
Captain Collingwood	George O'Brien
Lt. Collingwood	John Agar
Sergeant Mulcahy	Victor McLaglen
Mrs. Collingwood	Anna Lee
Mrs. O'Rourke	Irene Rich
Chief Cochise	Miguel Inclan
Quincannon	Dick Foran
Sergeant Shatuck	Jack Pennick
Dr. Wilkins	Guy Kibbee
Silas Meacham	Grant Withers
Martha	Mae March
Ma	Mary Gordon
Guadalupe	Movita
Southern recruit	Hank Worden
Recruit	Ray Hyke
Fen	Frances Ford

54

Adventure in Baltimore
RKO
Released: 1949
Running time: 89 minutes
Directed by Richard Wallace
CAST

Dinah Sheldon	Shirley Temple
Dr. Sheldon	Robert Young
Tom Wade	John Agar

Mr. Fletcher	Albert Sharpe
Mrs. Sheldon	Josephine Hutchinson
Mr. Steuben	Charles Kemper
Gene Sheldon	Johnny Sands
Mr. Eckert	John Miljan
H.H. Hamilton	Norma Varden
Bernice Eckert	Carol Brannan
Sis Sheldon	Patti Brady
Mark Sheldon	Gregory Marshall
Sally Wilson	Patsy Creighton

SHIRLEY TEMPLE GIFT CONTEST

Prizes That Would Make Lovely Christmas Presents Free For The Best Letters.

WE HAVE ascertained from many of our readers that mothers sometimes can only make their daughters willingly eat their spinach, or drink their milk, because Shirley Temple does so. Older sisters have often been able to teach younger ones the good manners and neatness required of them by setting Shirley up as an example. Teachers have also been aided in obtaining obedience from their little pupils by the same method. That is why we are here presenting an opportunity for you to write a letter telling us how Shirley Temple's influence has helped in the up-bringing of some little girl you know, to whom you would like to give a beautiful gift.

Pictured to the right is the first prize. This, as well as the second prizes, is the famous Shirley Temple doll coach made by the F. A. Whitney Carriage Company. All of them possess a white chassis, no nails visible on sides and no sharp edges—all rounded. They have one-piece French handles and non-pinching safety hood joints. On each side of the doll carriages there is a reproduction of Shirley's head, and her name appears on the hood knobs and wheel hub caps.

To make these doll carriages outstanding gifts, we have included with each one of them a Shirley Temple doll and a wool blanket with long fringe, embroidered with Shirley's name. A matching pillow completes the ensemble.

Shirley Temple photographed with the doll carriage, doll and accessories offered for the first prize.

Answer This Question And Win One Of These Beautiful Prizes:
How has Shirley Temple influenced the life of some little girl that you know?

FIRST PRIZE

A SHIRLEY TEMPLE doll carriage, 26" x 12½" with foot extension, and a 27 inch Shirley Temple baby doll. The carriage is fully upholstered with non-cracking leather cloth, has white enameled gear with shackle springs, 9" wire wheels and ¾" rubber tires. The baby doll is dressed in beautiful organdy clothes, with rubber panties. She has real blonde hair and real eyelashes, and cries when tipped forward or spanked. The doll represents Shirley Temple at the age of two. A wool blanket and matching pillow included.

TWELVE (12) SECOND PRIZES

SHIRLEY TEMPLE doll carriages, 19" x 9½", with 18 inch Shirley Temple baby dolls. Carriages have hoods of non-cracking leather cloth, plated safety joints, white enameled gears and handles, 7" wheels with ½" rubber tires. The dolls are the same as the first prize except in size. A wool blanket and matching pillow included.

EIGHTEEN (18) THIRD PRIZES

22 inch Shirley Temple dolls. These dolls are modeled after Shirley as she is today. They have long blonde curls and real eyelashes. The eyes not only open and close, but move from side to side—a feature no other doll has. The accordion pleated dresses that the dolls wear are attractive copies of Shirley Temple's own dress.

One of the third prize Shirley Temple dolls.

CONDITIONS

1. Your letter should not contain more than three hundred words.
2. Be sure your name and address appear on your letter.
3. Write your name and address plainly on the coupon below and attach it to your letter.
4. Neatness will be considered in awarding these prizes.
5. Contest closes midnight December 7, 1936.
6. Contest is opened to any reader with the exception of members of the staff of this magazine or their families.
7. In the event of ties the prize tied for will be sent to each tying contestant.
8. The prizes will be awarded for the most interesting letters in the opinion of the editor, whose decision will be final.

Editor,
   Shirley Temple Gift Contest,
     Silver Screen, 45 W. 45th St., New York, N. Y.
In the event that my letter is selected in this contest, I should be pleased to have the prize sent to me at the following address:

Name ....

Address ....

City .... State ....

55

Mr. Belvedere Goes To College
Twentieth Century Fox
Released: 1949
Running time: 82 minutes
Directed by Eliott Nugent
CAST

Lynn Belvedere —————————— Clifton Webb
Ellen Baker —————————— Shirley Temple
Bill Chase —————————— Tom Drake
Avery Brubaker —————————— Alan Young
Mrs. Chase —————————— Jessie Royce Landis
Kay Nelson —————————— Kathleen Hughes
Dr. Gibbs —————————— Taylor Holmes
Corny Whittaker —————————— Alvin Greenman
Dr. Keating —————————— Paul Harvey
Griggs —————————— Barry Kelly
Joe Fisher —————————— Bob Patten
Hickey —————————— Lee MacGregor
Marian —————————— Helen Westcott
Pratt —————————— Jeff Chandler
McCarthy —————————— Clancy Cooper
Sally —————————— Evelynn Eaton
Barbara —————————— Judy Brubaker
Babe —————————— Kathleen Freeman
Marta —————————— Lotte Stein
Jean Auchincloss —————————— Peggy Call
Nancy —————————— Ruth Tobey
Peggy —————————— Elaine Ryan
Isabelle —————————— Pattee Chapman
Fluffy —————————— Joyce Otis
Davy —————————— Lonnie Thomas
Prof. Ives —————————— Reginald Sheffield
Miss Cadwaller —————————— Katherine Lang
Mrs. Myrtle —————————— Isabel Withers
Instructor —————————— Arthur Space

56

The Story of Seabiscuit
Warner Brothers—First National
Released: 1949
Running time: 96 minutes
Directed by David Butler
CAST

Margaret O'Hara —————————— Shirley Temple
Shawn O'Hara —————————— Barry Fitzgerald
Ted Knowles —————————— Lon McCallister
Mrs. Charles S. Howard —————— Rosemary De Camp
George Carson —————————— Donald MacBride
Charles S. Howard —————————— Pierre Watkin
Thomas Miltford —————————— William Forrest
Murphy —————————— "Sugarfoot" Anderson
Jockey George Woolf —————————— Wm. J. Cartledge

57

A Kiss For Corliss
United Artists
Released: 1949
Running time: 88 minutes
Directed by Richard Wallace
CAST

Corliss Archer —————————— Shirley Temple
Kenneth Marquis —————————— David Niven
Mr. Archer —————————— Tom Tully
Mildred —————————— Virginia Welles
Dexter Franklin —————————— Darryl Hickman
Raymond Archer —————————— Robert Ellis
Taylor —————————— Richard Craig

Television Appearances

Shirley Temple's Storybook
NBC
January 12, 1958 to December 21, 1958
Hostess, narrator —————————— Shirley Temple

ABC
January 12, 1959 to December 21, 1959 (series re-aired)

Shirley Temple Theater
ABC
September 18, 1960 to September 10, 1961
Hostess, narrator —————————— Shirley Temple

Go Fight City Hall (proposed series/never released) 1961

Red Skelton April 1963

Mitch Miller 1964

Dinah Shore 1972

The Mike Douglas Show 1972

Shirley Temple

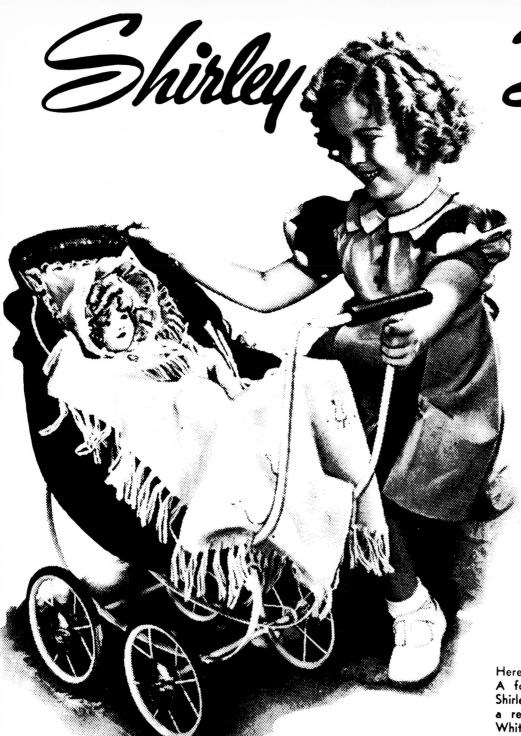

NEW FALL PROMOTION

- ● BABY DOLL
- ● DOLL CARRIAGE
- ● ROBE
- ● PILLOW

COMPLETE COMBINATION

$9.95 Retail

Here is a fall promotion that is "HOT". A four-item combination sale of Genuine Shirley Temple merchandise made to sell at a real bargain price. Offered jointly by Whitney and Ideal.

BABY DOLL BY IDEAL

Here is the genuine Shirley Temple Baby Doll. An exact image of Shirley at the age of 1 with her radiant smile, charming personality, cute dimples, eyes that flash and sparkle and flirt and sleep. Wig of real hair. Composition head, legs and arms. Kapok body with crying voice. Packed in a special Shirley Temple box with button and 8" x 10" picture suitable for framing.

IDEAL NOVELTY & TOY CO.
FACTORY: Long Island City
SALES OFFICE: 200 Fifth Avenue, New York City

COACH BY WHITNEY

Here is a genuine Shirley Temple Doll Coach with Shirley Temple picture on both sides. Her name on hood knobs and hub caps. A carriage every little girl will love. It has all white chassis. Entirely new construction features such as: no visible nails on sides, all rounded edges, hood joints that will not pinch little fingers.

F. A. WHITNEY CARRIAGE CO.
LEOMINSTER, MASS.

Write to either firm for prices and FREE MATS!

When writing to Ideal Novelty & Toy Co. or F. A. Whitney Carriage Co., will you please mention PLAYTHINGS?

With Painted Hair

With Wig

The Baby-SHIRLEY TEMPLE

NOW IN DOLL FORM

Here she is at the age of 2 before she set the world afire. Wasn't she a baby to hug? And won't little girls want to hug the life-like creation of their silver screen play-mate! Shirley Temple Baby Doll is **new**.

Baby Shirley has the new double-action glass eyes that flash and sparkle, sleep and flirt. She wears an organdy dress, underwear, socks and moccasins, and a bonnet comes in the gift box with the doll. Kapoc stuffed body, composition head, arms and legs, and a cry voice.

Each size packed in a special Shirley Temple box, bearing the little star's picture and signature confirming that it is the one and only Shirley Temple Doll. Each Doll wears a celluloid Shirley Temple button which her little mother can proudly wear to school.

AN 8X10 AUTOGRAPHED PHOTO OF SHIRLEY TEMPLE SUITABLE FOR FRAMING COMES WITH EACH DOLL.

OWN A BABY SHIRLEY TEMPLE DOLL TOO—AT ALL GOOD TOY STORES

SHIRLEY TEMPLE DOLL COSTUMES

Each outfit is individually packed in a white gift box bearing a large picture of the little star.

These beautiful costumes are all exact replicas of dresses worn by Shirley in her hit pictures.
Every genuine Shirley Temple doll garment is identified by a label bearing the signature of the little star.

Every little girl who has the doll will want one or more of these dresses.

ADD TO YOUR SHIRLEY TEMPLE DOLL'S WARDROBE. THESE ADORABLE CLOTHES OBTAINABLE AT YOUR TOY STORE.

SHIRLEY TEMPLE - RANGER DOLL or COWGIRL DOLL
Made in U.S.A.

HOTU-206

LARGE			MEDIUM			SMALL		
STYLE	**SIZE**		**STYLE**	**SIZE**		STYLE	SIZE	
No. 2027	27''		No. 2017	17''		No. 2011	11''	
QUANTITY	**PRICE**		**QUANTITY**	**PRICE**		QUANTITY	PRICE	
1 to 3	$15.98 ea.		1 to 6	$4.98 ea.		1 to 6	$2.98 ea.	
4 to 6	$12.00 ea.		7 to 11	$3.75 ea.		7 to 11	$2.25 ea.	
7 or more	$10.00 ea.		12 or more	$3.50 ea.		12 or more	$2.00 ea.	

Available in 3 sizes only at all 20th Century-Fox Exchanges

Chapter 5

Glossary of Terms

CASTILE SOAP. Popular brand name sold throughout the 1930s and 1940s. Used for bathing and washing clothes.

CELLULOID. A hard compound of cellulose nitrate and amphor used in manufacturing jewelry, imitation ivory, bone or coral. Doll companies began using celluloid in the manufacturing of pins and badges to label and identify dolls, beginning in the late 1800s.

COMPOSITION. Beginning sometime in the early 1900s, composition became a highly acceptable and very popular medium for manufacturing dolls. American companies soon became extremely competitive, each claiming to have their own superior secret formula. Composition consists of wood pulp (saw-dust) mixed with fillers such as chalk, clay, or whiting, bound with glue.

CRAZING. Hairline cracks that develop over time on glazed or painted surfaces. A direct result of sudden changes in temperature.

CRIER. Sound mechanism sewn inside the bodies of dolls and stuffed animals. A crying baby, "Ma Ma," and various animal bellows are most common. Operated by pressing or moving. Also known as the "voice box."

EDUCATIONAL FILM CORPORATION. Established by Earl Woolridge Hammons in 1919, it was originally based in New York City. Silent comedy shorts with Buster Keaton and Harry Langdon were their bread-and-butter. In Hollywood, they began producing short comedies featuring children in the hopes of competing with the *Our Gang Comedies*. The studio closed its doors, filing bankruptcy on September 28, 1933.

FLIRTY EYES. Eyes that move from side to side when the doll's head is turned by means of a weighted mechanism attached inside the head. Also known as "magic eyes" or "twinkle eyes."

FOX FILM CORPORATION. Founded by William Fox as a penny arcade during the early days of the nickelodeon. In 1912, Fox entered the production, distribution and exhibition business. The studio's first major star was the vampish screen siren Theda Bara. In 1935, Fox merged his company with Century Pictures, established two years earlier by Joseph M. Schenck and Darryl F. Zanuck. The new corporation was named Twentieth Century-Fox.

HIGH COLORING. Deep red blush painted on the cheeks, wrists, chest and knees.

HOLLYWOOD. The center of the American film industry. A section of Los Angeles, California named by Mrs. Deida Wilcox, the wife of a real estate broker who retired to a large ranch which she named "Hollywood." In 1891, the land began to slowly be subdivided, and the newly formed community was soon incorporated into a village retaining the name of the original ranch. In 1907, Col. William N. Selig moved his New York based motion picture studio west, to California, for its wide variety of terrains, vast open spaces and endless sunshine. Selig was followed quickly by film pioneers Cecil B. DeMille, Jesse Lasky and Samuel Goldwyn.

IDEAL NOVELTY AND TOY COMPANY. Founded in New York in 1902 by Morris Michtom, to manufacture teddy bears and stuffed toys. Under the control of his son, Benjamin F. Michtom, the 1930s found the company well-established and a leading doll and toy producer. Ideal is now a wholly-owned subsidiary of Tyco Toys, under the name of View-Master Ideal Group, Inc.

LOAN-OUT. A common motion picture studio practice where the services of an actor under contract are loaned to another studio for an agreed upon sum or trade.

MARKINGS. Raised letters or numbers found on the back of the head, just below the hair line, the upper back and sometimes on the inside of the arms and legs at the socket. Used to identify the manufacturer, name of the doll, size or mold number.

MOHAIR. The silky hair of the angora goat, commonly used in the manufacturing of doll wigs.

MOLD. Hollow form, usually made of metal or plaster, into which composition, porcelain, or wax is poured. Molds are used to press heads and body parts.

NOSTRILS. Composition dolls usually can be found with two red dots painted at the end of the nose to indicate nostrils.

N.R.A. The National Recovery Administration. Approved on June 16, 1933 as a part of the National Industrial Recovery Act during FDR's "New Deal" program. Established to combat the economic depression which followed the stock market crash of 1929. Designed to relieve unemployment by shortening labor hours, increasing wages and eliminating unfair trade practices and price cutting. The blue eagle emblem was adopted as their mark of identification and was placed on all goods manufactured under the code. The N.R.A. was dissolved on April 1, 1936 after the United States Supreme Court declared the act unconstitutional.

ORGANDY. A light and transparent muslin material.

OSCAR. First given in 1927 as the annual award of merit for motion picture artists and technicians by the Academy Of Motion Picture Arts and Sciences. It comes in the form of a 13½ inch gold-plated statue known as "Oscar." A special miniature version was presented to Shirley Temple in 1934. Other juvenile screen performers to receive the miniature statuette include; Mickey Rooney and Deanna Durbin in 1938, Judy Garland in 1939, Margaret O'Brien in 1944, Peggy Ann Garner in 1945, Bobby Driscoll in 1949, John Whitely in 1954 and Haley Mills in 1960.

PIQUE. Medium weight, crisp, cotton fabric with raised texture. Some patterns featured cords, waffle or bird's eye design.

PORCELAIN. Nonporous ceramic ware consisting of Kaolin clay, quartz and feldspar. China, bisque.

RAYON. Synthetic fibrous material. Imitation silk.

ROOTED HAIR. Small strands of hair that are pulled-up from inside of the head through a series of symmetrically placed holes.

SHORTS. Term applied to films consisting of only three reels or less, with a running time of under thirty minutes.

SLEEP EYES. Eyes that open and close. Eyes are attached to a thin metal framework inside of the head, with a hanging lead weight rocker. When the doll's head is upright (eyes open), the weight hangs down towards the chin area. When the doll is reclined, the weight of the rocker shifts to the back of the head, concealing the iris from view, giving the appearance of sleep. Eyes remain closed until the doll is again placed upright.

SYNTHETIC. Artificial. Not derived from nature.

VINYL. Man-made plastic material that is soft and pliable.

Shirley Temple

THE MOST WIDELY SOLD DOLL IN THE HISTORY OF THE WORLD

Shirley remains the biggest box-office name in the country. And the new Shirley Temple Doll is the favorite of all children.

As Shirley grows up so does her doll likeness. The new Shirley Temple Doll has the new hairdress that Shirley wears in her latest picture, and also her newest and finest dresses.

Here's the finest line of Shirley Temple Dolls that Ideal has ever made. In 7 different sizes, with Shirley's own winning smile, and cute dimples.

No.	Size Doll	Shipping Wt. (lbs.)	Retail ea.
2011	11"	1¼	$2.50
2013	13"	1½	3.00
2016	16"	2	4.00
2018	18"	3	5.00
2020	20"	3½	6.00
2022	22"	4½	7.00
2025	25"	6½	10.00
2027	27"	7½	12.00

Shirley Temple DOLLS

Here are the world's most adorable dolls—genuine Shirley Temple dolls—that every girl wants. Each doll has moving eyes—hazel, just like Shirley's. Each size is Shirley Temple to the life . . . with Shirley's winning smile, laughing eyes, cute dimple and natural golden hair worn as Shirley wears hers.

BEAUTIFULLY DRESSED

Each doll is dressed in authentic copies of the clothes Shirley wears in her "hit" pictures. Each doll wears the authentic Shirley Temple button and comes in special Shirley Temple gift box with the little star's autographed photo, suitable for framing.

Keeping Shirley Curly!

A fascinating new Play Feature has been added to bring new appeal and greater popularity to the new Shirley Temple dolls for 1938. There is no other doll in the world like the Shirley Temple doll, for only these genuine new Shirley Temple dolls have ENOUGH hair and GOOD ENOUGH hair to be waved, curled and set in different ways by industrious little mothers. "Keeping Shirley Curly" is the new Play Feature that every girl will adore. With every Shirley Temple doll you get Shirley Temple doll hair curlers and instructions, enabling little girls to keep their dolls' hair waved and curled in the latest Hollywood styles.

3 STYLES — 4 SIZES

As shown below, three styles of Shirley Temple dolls are offered. Shirley in her party dress and Shirley in her dancing dress come in four sizes. Shirley in her Wee Willie Winkie costume comes in just one size. Each doll is all composition with naturally shaped body and limbs fully jointed. The eyes have true-to-life curly lashes, and go to sleep when you lay the darling down. And—each Shirley Temple doll now comes with curlers and instructions for keeping Shirley curly. Only these Shirley Temple dolls have enough hair and good enough hair to be waved and curled just like Shirley Temple's own hair!

SHIRLEY'S NEWEST DRESSES

SHIRLEY'S PARTY DRESS

Shirley Temple doll offered in four sizes. The party dress is fine white figured organdy, with silk ribbon hand bow, three heart-shaped buttons. The doll closes her eyes and goes to sleep when you put her to bed. The 27-inch doll has eyes that also move from side to side. Hair curlers included.

H26256	Size 13 in.	$ 4.50
H26257	Size 18 in.	7.45
H26258	Size 22 in.	10.00
H26259	Size 27 in.	16.50

SHIRLEY'S DANCING DRESS

Shirley is the best little dancer the screen has known! This is an adorable outfit she is wearing, a dancing dress of fine organdy, accordian pleated. Silk ribbons at the wrists enable the doll to hold the dress up in fancy ballet posture. Choice of four sizes each with sleeping eyes. The 27-inch doll has eyes that also move from side to side. Each doll has the curlers that enable you to keep Shirley curly.

H26252	Size 13 in.	$ 4.50
H26253	Size 18 in.	7.45
H26254	Size 22 in.	10.00
H26255	Size 27 in.	16.50

"WEE WILLIE WINKIE"

Shirley Temple doll with Glen Garry costume. An exact copy of the beautiful costume that Shirley wears in her latest and greatest success "Wee Willie Winkie." This doll comes in just the 18-inch size, the most popular size. Note from the large true-to-life photo of Shirley above at the right, how perfectly the doll's costume reproduces Shirley's original! Like the other Shirley Temple dolls, this model has hazel eyes with curly lashes and comes complete with curlers. When you lay her down, the doll closes her eyes and gently goes to sleep. She's the cutest doll imaginable, with the loveliest curls, the merriest smile, and the most charming personality!

H26260 PRICE.................$8.95

"WEE WILLIE WINKIE"
Shirley's Greatest Picture

America's Number One sweetheart—Shirley Temple—has scored her biggest success in her latest picture "Wee Willie Winkie." If you haven't yet seen this production, be sure to watch for it—it's well worth waiting for!

In "Wee Willie Winkie," Shirley has given the grandest performance of her career. Starred with such experienced players as Victor McLaglen, June Lang, C. Aubrey Smith and Michael Whalen, Shirley has done full justice to Rudyard Kipling's immortal tale.

Shirley Temple dolls reproduce Shirley's winning smile, her laughing eyes, and natural curly hair. Each doll wears a Shirley Temple button. You have your choice of three costumes as shown at the left. They are perfect reproductions of the dresses Shirley wore in her most successful pictures. Every girl wants a Shirley Temple Doll—and now every girl can have the fun of keeping her Shirley curly!

Early Shirley catalog advertisement ca. 1937, courtesy Marge Meisinger.

Price Guide

Condition, desirability, rarity, visual appeal, original clothing and size are the key factors which determine price. Condition is always of major importance and should be a top priority when purchasing any doll.

With the recent sky-rocketing prices of antique and collectible dolls, obtaining an original 1930s Shirley Temple doll can mean a sizeable investment. Minor wear, such as small paint-rubs on the nose, fingertips, eyelashes, lips, or around the arm and leg sockets, usually can be expected and most often do not effect the overall value of a composition doll. However, whenever possible, avoid paying top prices for dolls with cracking, crazing, lifting of the paint finish, or dolls that have been rewigged, repainted or redressed. When buying with the intention of a possible future resale, remember, originality is far more desirable than any replacement, painted or otherwise.

All original dolls, either of exceptionally high quality, mint condition, in original box or trunk, or a doll wearing one of the more rare outfits, will always bring a premium price well above the book value. Additionally, the smallest size composition Shirley Temple doll at 11 inches (28cm) and the largest size of 27 inches (69cm), also command a higher price as fewer examples of these dolls were manufactured, thus increasing their desirability.

The following prices have been evaluated using the criteria listed above and are based upon current prices realized at auction houses and in the collector's marketplace. Neither the author nor the publisher assume any responsibility for losses incurred as a result of using this guide. Prices listed are not intended to set prices, but to simply and ONLY act as a guide.

Page	Position	Price Range	Page	Position	Price Range
7	C	$1000 & up	22	TR	$300-400
9	C	$10-12	23	L	$700-750
10	C	$10-12	23	R	$750-850
12	C	$10-12	25	T	$200-250 each
14	CL	$650-675	26	L	$150-200
14	CR	$700-750	26	R	$175-225
14	BL	$750-800	27	C 8"	$35-45 each
14	BR	$800-850	27	C 12"	$45-55 each
15	C	$750-850	28	T	$240
17	TL	$5-10 each	29	C	$10-12
17	BL	$25-30	30	C	$10-12
17	R	$900-1000	31	C	$10-12
18	T	$900-1000	32	C	$700-750
18	BL	$85 each	33	C Doll	$600-650
18	BR	$100-125 each	33	C Trunk	$150-200
19	C	$25-35	33	C Outfits	$100 & up each
20	BL	$500-600	34	L	$900 & up
20	BR	$850 & up	34	R	$900 & up
21	TR Ideal	$850 & up	33	TR	$10-12
21	TR Alexander	$500-600	35	B	$100 & up
21	B	$200 & up	36	TL	$100 & up
22	TL	$250-275	36	BL	$100 & up

36	R	$650-700		58	TL Hanger	$25-30
37	C	$10-12		58	CL	$800-900
38	BL	$850 & up		58	TR	$700-750
38	R	$10-12		58	BR	$650-700
39	CL	$850 & up		59	TL	$700-800
39	BR	$200 & up		59	BL	$650-725
40	L	$10-12		59	R	$10-12
40	R	$700-750		60	TL	$750-800
41	TL Dress	$100 & up		60	BL	$100 & up
41	TL Hanger	$25-30		60	TR	$600-650
41	BL	$700-750		60	BR	$650-725
41	R	$700-750		61	TL	$600-650
42	TL	$750-850		61	TR Doll	$700-750
42	BL	$100 & up		61	TR Trunk	$150-200
42	BR	$10-12		61	TR Dress	$100 & up
43	TC Doll	$1000 & up		61	B	$100 & up each
43	TC Trunk	$150-200		62	TL Outfit	$100 & up
43	BR	$850 & up		62	TL Hanger	$25-30
44	TL	$850 & up		62	BL	$600-650
44	BL 20"	$1000 & up		62	R	$10-12
44	BL 13"	$850 & up		63	TL	$650-700
44	CR Rabbit	$150-200		63	BL	$100 & up each
44	CR Doll	$1000 & up		63	TR	$100 & up
45	BL	$1500 & up		63	BR	$100 & up
45	R	$10-12		64	TL	$100 & up
46	L	$10-12		64	BL	$750-850
46	TR Dress	$100 & up		64	BR	$900-1000
46	TR Hanger	$25-30		65	TL	$850-950
46	BR Dress	$100 & up		65	BL	$40-50
46	BR Hanger	$25-30		65	R	$10-12
47	L	$10-12		66	TL	$1000 & up
47	TR	$700-750		66	BR	$800-900
47	BR	$700-750		67	TL	$650-675
48	L	$750 & up		67	BL Dress	$100 & up
48	TR	$700-750		67	BL Hanger	$25-30
48	BR	$600-700		67	TR	$650-750
49	TL	$700-750		67	BR Dress	$150 & up
49	BL	$700-750		67	BR Hanger	$25-30
49	RC	$700-750		68	BL 17"Ranger	$750-850
50	L	$10-12		68	BL 18" Wee Willie	$1000 up
50	TR	$700-750		68	BL 16" Ranger	$750-850
50	BR	$850-900		68	TR	$1000 & up
51	BL	$100 & up		69	C	$1200 & up
51	R	$10-12		70	CL	$100 & up
52	BL	$750-800		70	TR	$100 & up
52	R	$10-12		70	B	$50-100 each
53	TL	$400 & up		71	TC	$100 & up
53	BR	$10-12		71	BL	$1000 & up
54	L	$1000-1100		71	BR	$100 & up
54	R	$900-1000		72	TL	$125 & up
55	R	$10-12		72	BL	$600-650
56	BL	$800-850		72	TR	$100 & up
56	TR	$650-675		72	BR	$100 & up
56	BR	$800-850		73	T	$10-12
57	TL	$750-850		73	BR Doll	$700-750
57	R	$10-12		73	BR Figurine	$100-135
58	TL Dress	$100 & up		74	TL	$750-850

74	TR	$60-80
74	B	$700-750 each
75	T 20"	$1000 & up
75	T 18"	$700-750
75	T 17"	$750-850
75	T 16"	$650-675
75	T 13"	$850 & up
75	T 11"	$700-750
75	BL	$25-30
75	BR Outfits	$100 up each
75	BR Trunk	$150-200
75	BR Shoes/skates	$25-35 each
76	TL	$250-300
76	BL	$75-100
76	TR	$225-250
76	BR	$75-100
77	TL	$250-300
77	TR	$50-60
77	B	$200-250 each
78	TL	$200-250
78	C	$250-275
78	CR	$250-275
78	BL	$25-35 each
79	TC	$300-350
79	BL	$350-400
79	TR	$325-350
79	BR Wrist tag	$25-35
80	L	$325-350
80	TR	$375-400
80	BR	$325-350
81	TL	$75-100
81	TR	$50-75
81	B	$100-150
82	TL	$50-75
82	BL	$50-75
82	TR	$50-75
83	TL	$50-75
83	BL	$50-75
83	TR	$50-75
83	BR	$50-75
83	C	$50-75
84	TL	$50-75
84	BL	$50-75
84	TR	$50-75
84	BR	$50-75
85	T	$50-75
85	B	$50-75
86	TL	$50-75
86	BL	$50-75
86	TR	$50-75
86	BR	$50-75
87	TL Boxes	$40-60 each
87	BL	$35-45
87	TR	$50-75
87	BR	$35-45
88	TL	$35-45
88	BL	$40-50

88	TR	$35-45
88	BR 8"	$35-45
88	BR 12"	$45-55
89	T	Cut $95 Uncut $150
89	B	Cut $95 Uncut $150
90	TL Boxed	$125
90	BL	$25
90	TR	$45
91	TL	$25-30
91	BL	$75-85
91	TR	$75-85
92	TCB	$15-20
93	T	$25
93	BL	$15
93	BR	$20
94	TL	$25
94	BL	$25
94	TR	$25
94	BR	$35
95	T	$55
95	B Boxed	$125-150
96	TL	$45
96	TR	$85-100
96	B Boxed	$125
97	TL	$50-75
97	CL	$50-75
97	BL	$30
97	TR	$50-75
97	BR	$50-75
98	T	$50-75
98	BL	$55
98	BR	$45
99	TL	$45
99	BL	$55
99	TR	$45
99	BR	$35
100	TL	$45
100	CL	$50
100	TC	$55
100	C	$25
100	TR	$55
100	CR	$35
101	TL Left	$15
101	TL Right	$15
101	B	$25-35
102	CL	$150
102	TR	$125-150
102	CR	$15
102	BR	$35
103	TL	$35
103	BL	$45
103	CR	$45
104	L	$150-175
104	TR	$150
105	TL	$35 each
105	BL	Mint $45-50 each
105	TR	$35

105	BR	$60
106	TL	$3-5
106	CR	$45
106	BC	$45
107	T	$45
107	C	$35
107	B	$35
108	TL	$75-100
108	BL	$100-150
108	TR	$50-60
108	BR	$25-35
109	TL	$30-40
109	BL	$25
109	TR	$50
109	BR	$25
110	TL Doll	$1300-1400
110	TL Hat	$45-60
110	BL	$15-20 each
111	TL	$75-100
111	BL	$75-100
111	TR	$75-100
111	BR	$75-100
111	C	$75-100